How To Get Your Husband To Fulfill Your Emotional Needs

Margaret Hardisty

HARVEST HOUSE PUBLISHERS
Irvine, California 92714

**HOW TO GET YOUR HUSBAND
TO FULFILL YOUR EMOTIONAL NEEDS**

Copyright © 1980 by Harvest House Publishers
Irvine, California 92714

Library of Congress Catalog Card Number 80-81471
ISBN 0-89081-249-7

Printed in the United States of America.

I dedicate this book to

Bessie E. Greene

My Mother

who taught me that I shouldn't
settle for less than to be treated as
a very special person by the men in my life

FOREWORD

The man to whom I have been married for 22 years is romantic, loving, thoughtful, a good provider, a dandy father, tender, a terrific leader, a super helper, and one who commands my respect in almost everything. For a woman who had planned never to get married in the first place (because I preferred a career to being a slave to a man or his house) that's quite an admission.

But if I am to be perfectly honest, I also have to admit that within his masculine breast lurks the potential for some not-so-delightful qualities which, had they found complete freedom of expression, might have reduced me to what would have resembled grated cheese.

He and I have worked hard to keep that from happening, for we both have realized that he isn't the only one who is a special, unique person, but I am too! We both know that I could not be the kind of wife he needs, and he could not be the kind of husband I need, and neither of us could be the kind of mates God wants us to be, if either of us became merely an extension of the other.

In order for him to ACT upon what he and I discovered, I had to take seriously my role of ''helper,'' as designed by God (recorded in Genesis 2:18), by *helping* my man understand

WHAT I needed from him, HOW he could supply it, and WHY it would benefit him in the long run.

Some of my helping techniques, as well as those of dozens of other happily married women, are revealed in this book, so that you too can be assured of admiration, respect, and adoration from your husband, which can result in your romantic and emotional needs being supplied, if you utilize them. You can move into that enviable position without loss of self-worth, and certainly without trying to manipulate the one you love.

—Margaret Hardisty

CONTENTS

1

EXPECT A RAINBOW!

◆——————————————————————————

Got a problem which centers around your husband? Perhaps your difficulty is the same as Lisa's. Her man wouldn't do anything with his dirty socks except let them perfume the floor. She talked it over with him calmly. No change. She bawled him out angrily. He just laughed. She appealed to his sense of manhood. He was unimpressed.

"The trouble with you is," a friend advised, "that you are forgetting your role as a submissive, loving wife. You should be picking up the socks yourself with a cheerful attitude."

But Lisa couldn't quite swallow the idea of encouraging what she felt was her husband's immature behavior, so she had a think time with herself and decided to try one other approach. It worked. Beautifully!

Or maybe you can better identify with Betty. Her Romeo seemed to think she was just a body for him to use whenever he wished. Sweet thoughtfulness had become almost nonexistent. "Where did the romance go?" she cried. But rather than continuing to cry, she decided to do something about it, and she did. Successfully!

Then again you might have a little boy in men's clothing who spends every cent that crosses his palm, playing havoc with the budget and tempting bill collectors to ring your phone off the hook. Corrine struggled with that one for awhile, and then—the answer to her dilemma was there.

Whatever clouds are pouring down on your picnic, you can make sure a rainbow breaks through. You just might see that man of yours straighten away and become the dream you thought he was going to be when you consented to marry him.

And while you are reading *how,* you'll also find out what Lisa, Betty, Corrine, and others have done to bring about a change of attitude in their husbands toward dirty socks, forgotten romance, slaphappy spending, and many other irritating difficulties.

The Number One Query

More than any other question, I am asked by women across the nation, "How can I get my husband to be concerned about my emotional needs?" The frequency with which this question is asked indicates that, despite the fact that most women claim they know their men inside and out, the male gender tends to puzzle and exasperate the opposite sex more than the ladies like to admit. For example,

WHO BUT A HUSBAND . . .

. . . insists he can listen to you at the same time he reads the newspaper, but doesn't hear a word you say?

. . . expects you to be almost perfect but feels threatened if you come near to it?

. . . bawls out the kids if he hears they didn't pay attention in school, but nods through the pastor's sermon?

. . . shouts a stubborn "No!" when you want to do something he's sure you shouldn't, and then, when you're out of the mood six months later, suggests that you do it?

. . . takes one look at you after you've fixed up from head to toe for him and asks, "What's for dinner?"

. . . is sure that there's no way you can accomplish a goal you've set and then nods his head in a disinterested fashion when you reach it?

. . . worries you by working too hard but relaxes when you desperately need his help?

. . . urges you to get a job so you'll feel fulfilled and independent, and then holds his hand out for your paycheck because he doesn't think you can handle the spending of it?

. . . gives a lecture to the family about being content under all circumstances, but paces back and forth if he has to wait three minutes longer to leave because his wife is finishing washing the car, which he didn't do because he was watching the football game?

. . . insists that the children behave themselves at the table and then drinks his soup from the bowl?

. . . yells angrily at you because you didn't balance your checkbook properly and then expects you to be ready for sex a half-hour later?

. . . is too tired to take out the garbage but becomes a ball of energy if a good-looking woman drops in to visit?

. . . jumps impulsively into a foolish decision and then, realizing it was a mistake, lectures his wife thus: "*We* have a tendency to rush into things sometimes. *We* really blew it this time"?!!!

Cold Potatoes

If wishes were horses and beggars could ride, I might wish that I could go on to temper that list by making the sweeping statement, "Oh well, no matter how much they might cause life to be a bit of a challenge for a wife, when it all comes out in the Monday wash, husbands are usually kind, a joy, comforting, adorable, anxious to be thoughtful, attentive, and willing to change almost anything in order to make their wives happy." But it gets stuck in my teeth like a marshmallow, because too many wives unite their thoughts in chorus and succinctly agree that plenty of men are like cold potatoes. They need to have a fire built under them to get them moving.

Although there are some husbands who are a delight to their spouses, and mine is one of them, too many husbands seem unable to understand wives' needs and won't do much about them if they do. Whether they have emotional hangups from childhood, are reacting to environmental pressures, or are just lazy or unfeeling doesn't change the fact that Milady is unhappy in more ways than one, and needs to see something take place other than what has become daily fare.

Recently I read a book about a world-renowned personality and her equally famous husband. Nobody seemed to really know if the lady knew that her husband was having sexual liaisons with dozens upon dozens of women, the book said. Later on it was concluded that she did indeed know but found it expedient and to her own best interests to ignore them.

That's fine with me. If, for whatever reason, a woman wants to put up with her present situation rather than help her husband improve morally or spiritually to change a marriage for the better, who am I to complain on her behalf?

But if you have decided that you might like to consider the alternative, and if you are ready to quit apologizing mentally for being a woman, then let's move on.

Clever Women

In answer to a letter which I sent out to a number of men, asking for their insight into the matter of uncooperative husbands, one stated, "There is nothing one person can do to change another."

Although in some cases this seems to be true, my files are full of letters and accounts of personal discussions with men and women which attest exactly the opposite. Everyone who comes into your life affects your thinking or behavior in some way. Without even trying, we influence others to change all the time. Many men have told me that if their wives had not taken persistent, affirmative action, their marriages either wouldn't have made it or they wouldn't be as happy as they are now. That action in some cases was passive and in other cases active.

When talking with women who seemingly have successful marriages, I find that once we break through the answers they feel they are *expected* to give, and they realize that it won't make them appear unspiritual or less than what they should be to deviate from those answers, they reveal that they've been very busy about the business of influencing their husbands not only to supply their needs as wives, but also to be better fathers and a host of other goodies.

Every Woman's Dream?

One time after we were interviewed on national TV, two women who had been in the audience gushed cheerfully to my husband, "We'd like to take you home with us." Many times I am asked by readers, "Is your husband really that perfect?" Men have confessed jokingly to me that they'd like to punch George in the nose for setting such a lofty example for them to follow.

But he didn't become that way by inheritance. I've had plenty of gripes over the years, and some of the things I've written about reflect them. As George often tells our audiences, "I've learned a lot about my wife and myself since she started writing." Without a doubt, from the beginning of our marriage, he has been doing plenty to help me conquer weaknesses of mine so we could be happier together. but so have I been doing plenty to help him conquer weakness of his so we could be happier together.

Not Always A Featherbed

Granted, the way to marital bliss is not easy, especially in view of the fact that husbands, bless them, can be as immovable as a stone quarry. But remember that even stone quarries have been used bit by bit to build beautiful palaces, provided the stonecutter is patient and skilled in his work.

If you want to blow bubbles, you have to chew the gum. If you want to have riches, you generally can't count on a distant uncle leaving you his millions. Nor does a happy, joyful relationship with someone just happen! If that's what you want with the one you call Sweetheart, or at least *used* to call Sweetheart, you're going to have to pay the price of putting effort into getting it to that point.

Sweet Determination

I was intrigued watching a deep-blue-and-black butterfly one afternoon. She had landed on a pink stock that had seen better days. But she knew that somewhere in those dilapidated blossoms was some nectar, and she was going to get it out. She moved around to each side of the source of her interest, using her extracting apparatus efficiently. A breeze stiff enough to tug her off into the air puffed at her intermittently, but she hung on tenaciously. At last, amply rewarded for her efforts, she released her hold, lifted into the sunshine, and rather drunkenly floated first one way and then another, exulting in her triumph.

Somewhere down inside that masculine heart of your man are some lovely qualities that haven't shown themselves yet. Just as the moth determined to achieve victory, so must you, keeping in mind that the honey which eventually will bubble to the surface will sweeten his life, your life, and the lives of your children.

Achieving anything of worth takes plenty of ladylike perspiration and a terrific use of physical, emotional, mental, and spiritual fortitude. If in the past you have gotten your nose bumped a few times, and if part of what you built fell down on top of you, leaving a pile of bruises and discouragement, lift the stones off, struggle to your feet, shake yourself vigorously, apply medicine if needed, put a smile on your face, and say, "So what?!" Get yourself moving and be on your way. If the rosebushes of love turned out to have some very nasty thorns on them, get out of the rose garden and try the daisy bed instead. Go a different route. Come in from a different angle. If your first foundation had a lot of sand in it and is thus collapsing, get busy building another.

Divorce?

If you think I'm offering license for you to shed the shackles of your present marriage altogether, I am not. You *might* be able to be happier with someone else. I've seen some happy second marriages. Many people try harder the second time around. Happiness with a second mate is not guaranteed, however. In their February 11, 1980, issue, *Newsweek* notes that the rate of divorce in second marriages is 40 percent. That's 7 percent higher than the rate for first marriages. Too often a lady will jump out of the too-hot frying pan right into a hotter fire, since she tends to be attracted to the same type of man or she finds out, too late, that her new hubby has pretended to be something entirely different from what he is, to the devastation of their relationship later on. Furthermore, the strain of searching for unity in a situation where stepparents and children are involved is very often untenable. And who's to say you could even *find* another husband?

Women so outnumber men that in the marriage business it's a man's market.

One fact that no one can get around, except through rationalization, is that, even though *some* women remarry and seem to be happier than the first time around, the children whose lives are shattered by divorce are not. We cited a few convincing facts in our book *How to Enrich Your Marriage,* including reference to a secular write-up of a study done on children of divorced couples. The picture was not pretty. The aforementioned *Newsweek* article revealed that children who have to tolerate their parents' missteps suffer depression, a feeling of rejection, a desire to bully, shock, fear, and a host of other destructive symptoms. Boys sometimes take on feminine characteristics due to the absence of the father, which might be saying a lot about the spreading of homosexuality today.

Running away from problems in a marriage by getting divorced can start a snowball-plummeting-down-a-mountain effect. One woman who heard me speak at a retreat followed me from one speaking engagement to another. Finally, when my husband and I were conducting a marriage seminar, she brought her mate along. Counseling with them revealed that, although she was in her early thirties, this was her fifth marriage and her husband's third. She had given birth to three children from her former unions. Her present husband had two of his own children living with them. They had also taken in two other youngsters, one of which was the son of one of her former mates . . . the other, a niece.

For the finishing touch, they were each

demanding so much of the other that their present relationship was about to self-destruct. It might be interesting to see what happens to the children in that family in years to come as they try to make sense out of their world of the blind leading the blind!

If all the facts I've stated thus far haven't convinced you, I might add that I cannot find anything in the Holy Scriptures which gives you a moral or spiritual right to *initiate* divorce, expect possibly if your husband has committed adultery.

Heart Check

If there are dark feelings rumbling around inside, away with them! On with happy, positive thinking! You have an invitation to embark upon a very challenging adventure. If you want a love that endures, climb on board, roll up your sleeves, and set into motion your lovely feminine ability to reason. Join me as we begin to draw up the plan for a castle that your king will be glad you encouraged him to help you build.

2

LET'S STOP
FIGHTING WINDMILLS

◆──────────────────────────────

Before we leap into some very practical steps that you can take to improve your present situation, we must clear some murky air and reach a few understandings about three very important terms that have been bandied about with little understanding as to their true meanings: *manipulation, game-playing,* and *submission.* If these are not important to average Mrs. America, they are certainly of vital importance to Mrs. Christian America, for she generally desires, deep inside, to be pleasing to God and to her husband, and that is as it should be.

There are many women out there who have been computerized to believe that they mustn't do *anything* to influence Husband to reconsider the way he has been acting toward Wife year after year. They are told that if they do, they are practicing manipulation—a dirty word—and are *not* practicing submission (the golden privilege). However, they have been fed false information. They need to strike over the error and substitute a proper perspective.

So let's cast aside our fears and sift through cultural prejudice and slanted biblical teaching to find out what's really truth and what isn't. It's the only way we can lay a foundation of self-worth that is necessary in order to build that castle of a dream marriage.

Manipulation

We are so gun-shy about manipulation (due, perhaps, to the popularity of writings on it these days) that it seems we sometimes even label common sense with it. Sometimes those who are loudly warning all within hearing about the evils of manipulation are like Don Quixote, who, as you will recall from your high school English days, imagined windmills to be giants and took to fighting them vigorously. Let's not make the same mistake.

I have discussed the term with several psychologists and marriage counselors. Although each gave his or her variety of definition, all seem to agree that *manipulation has the implication of scheming or doing something underhandedly to get someone to do something we want for ourselves with little or no thought for what good it will do the other person.* That puts the dragon in another pasture, doesn't it?

I'd be naive if I said that there are no wives who practice manipulation on a regular basis in order to line their own jewel cases, to get sympathy, to move into a position of power, or for some other unhealthy motivation. There *are* women like that. Betty was one of them.

When Betty was a child, she was ill a great deal and received a lot of special privileges. Her unloving, bullyish father and her uninterested mother wouldn't punish her like they did the other children. In fact, her two brothers and her sister were expected to tend to her needs. When in the hospital, nurses would cater to the ". . . cute little thing." She began to associate sickness with getting love and attention.

When Betty married, she wanted special attention from her husband, and later, from the children that were born to them, but found that they didn't respond to her demanding. So she would take to her sickbed. From that lofty throne she could dispense her orders, and if the family wasn't cooperative, or wearied of it, she would become *very* ill so she would have to be rushed to the hospital.

Her desire to be ill actually made her that way a good deal of the time, so she could legitimately rule her household into dancing attendance on her. Actually the family didn't mind too much, for when she was sick she was laughing, jovial, and fun. When she was up and around, her amiableness turned to harsh discipline, criticism, or yelling.

The day came when Betty decided, after many years, not to be sick anymore, but not until she had lost three husbands in divorce.

Betty's desire for love and attention wasn't unnecessarily abnormal, but her method of achieving them was unhealthy and manipulative, as she found out with professional help from a Christian psychologist.

Maurine is a manipulator too. She likes diamonds and expensive gold jewelry. Although her husband makes good money, her spending stretches his ability to keep up at times. To pay the bills which she runs up to indulge her appetite, he has to work long hours, which leaves him little leisure time. When he asked her not to charge anymore, she took money out of their savings, without his knowledge, to pay for her latest purchases. Recently, tired of it all, he filed for divorce.

Liking diamonds and gold jewelry was not necessarily wrong. What *was* wrong was that Maurine had only one person's interests in mind—her own. She didn't care a whisper about the physical and emotional needs of her husband, nor did she hesitate to act underhandedly to achieve her goals.

The way these two women operated was a lot different from trying to get someone to do something so *he* will benefit, and taking steps to ensure the doing. Even God uses that method with His children. Although we receive salvation free of strings attached, we are promised rewards *if* we do this or that, and problems *if* we don't.

So now that we know what real manipulation is, we don't need to feel guilty any longer about doing something we weren't doing in the first place.

Game Playing

Like the term "manipulation," those who decry the evils of "game-playing" in human relationships put the label on practically any attempt to be nice, including graciousness and thoughtfulness. Trying to communicate in such a way that someone else is made more comfortable or happy makes one suspect.

Pleasing others and drawing the best response from them can be as fun as looking for a new dress! If your intent is sincere, forget that falsely labeled destroyer of feminity, "game-playing," and get on with being a human being.

Submission—What It Is Not

Just as Don Quixote took on flocks of sheep as well as windmills, convinced that they were enemy armies, so swords are being thrashed about in panic in an effort to destroy what is thought of as lack of submission of wives to husbands.

As a result of a culturally stereotyped definition of submission, many men are frustrated and confused as their women fail to fit into that definition. Many make a valiant attempt to do so, however. One such lady came up to me at a ladies' retreat, just after I had given a message on a wife's responsibilities to help her husband supply her emotional needs so they would both benefit.

"Did I understand you to say that women should be submissive to their husbands?" she queried.

"Yes," I answered, "but of course, we have to understand what being submissive means."

She raised one eyebrow and said, "I think it means just what it says. A woman should let her husband do anything with her that he wants, even it it means she must be a doormat to him. She should obey him without question—about everything."

I took up the challenge, for by this time we had a knot of women gathered around us, listening.

"If your husband asked you to murder someone, would you do it?"

She flushed and stammered, "Th . . . that's different. That would be disobeying God."

"I agree," I agreed. "Does it follow, then, that a woman would be disobeying God by aiding her husband in committing a crime by, say, allowing him to beat her, since it is against the law?"

She had no immediate comeback, so I continued, "And isn't there a possibility that a woman would be helping her husband disobey God is she didn't encourage him to supply her emotional needs as God has commanded him to do?"

She smiled, thanked me for being there, and went on her way. Whether she was merely being solicitous of my radicalism, or agreeing with me, I don't know.

Her brand of submission might better be called "submersion." It saddles women with a purple cow that gives yellow-gray milk that turns the stomach and leaves them with a heavy guilt when they don't want to drink it.

I'd like to have a ten-dollar bill for every woman I have encountered who has used the submersive type of "submission" to the point that she destroyed her marriage altogether. I'd have a fat bank account if I did.

A lady in whose home we stayed when ministering in Oklahoma is a classic example. She confided in me that she knows that the reason she lost her husband was because she was determined to be a totally submissive, obedient wife—submissive and obedient after the fashion of cultural teaching. She said, "In trying to be the perfect wife and letting him know I considered him head of the house, I expected him to make all the decisions and became totally dependent on him. I was there for him to wipe his feet on if he wished. I jumped to grant his slightest wish. I agreed with everything he said. I never suspected he was getting sick of it. One day he simply walked out and got a divorce. There was no other woman involved at the time. He told me that he had lost all respect for me and that I bored him to death. Two years later he married whom I thought was my best friend. I believed I was doing what God commands. Now I know I misunderstood."

An experienced wife informed Adelle, "When you are out with your husband, you are too outgoing and he is too quiet. You must be the quiet one. Don't talk very much. You are a leader, but you shouldn't be. Quit teaching Sunday school. Take charge of nothing. Get him to do it instead."

Meanwhile, that wife's husband got to Adelle's Ronald with, "Take charge! Your wife is a leader. She has to quit that. You have to let her know who's boss all the time."

Ronald, wanting to do what was right, forced himself to move into a different role. He would allow Adelle no discussion regarding any decision. He exploded, "I didn't ask you if you should quit teaching. I said it. That's final! If anyone teaches, I will! From now on, I'll tell you what you'll do and what you won't."

They were both trying to change their basic personalities. What poor advice they had been given! How often it brings tragic results. Since he discovered that he taught about as well as she could do the plumbing, and the unnatural roles they were being asked to play suited neither of them, they soon made adjustments before too much unhappiness resulted.

Somebody Made A Mistake

God is not the one who is in error. His type of submission works! It produces happy wives and happy husbands. The difficulty arises when we get off-target in understanding the implications of the term, and sometimes the reason we get off-target is because there's another half to the problem that isn't considered in its entirety at all. That half is the husband's responsibilities toward the wife as outlined by God. Once the husband fulfills his responsibilities and the woman responds by fulfilling hers, the puzzle begins to fit together in a most beautiful and understandable way.

A Divinely Initiated Plan!

Our heavenly Father is not devoid of common sense or understanding, although to hear and read some of the restrictions we impose on others, "backing it up" with Scripture, you'd almost think so.

Way back in the beginning, God introduced breathtakingly lovely Eve to her incredulous husband, because Adam needed someone to help him . . . help him be content . . . help him tend the garden . . . help him be less lonely. If Adam and Eve had never disobeyed God, their relationship would have remained uncomplicated. But as soon as sin came, disorder and chaos resulted in their lives and their hearts.

Therefore, God appointed Adam some additional chores that have been man's heritage ever since. The divine edict says that the husband is to lead his family unit with wisdom, providing for them spiritually, physically, and emotionally.

Part of this means, we are told, that he is to love his wife as he loves his own body— honoring her, understanding her, and treating her as Christ treats the church. A Christian calls upon Jesus Christ when she needs something, does she not? And what does our Lord do? He becomes her servant! He answers that prayer! He may say "No" or "Wait a bit," or He may say "Yes." But whatever His decision, that child of His knows that it was made with her best interests in mind. So is a husband to treat his wife.

He is to listen to her, trust her, allow her to have a *big* say in family decisions, respect and admire her, and teach the children to do likewise.

If Mr. Head-of-the-Wife doesn't do all these things, he just might find that his prayers go no further than the ball in a tennis match. God meant for His orders to be carried out. (Relevent Scripture verses are listed at the back of this book.)

Essential You!

All of that puts your husband in a very important position! But he needn't fold under the weight of it. He's got a top-notch helper—you! God knows that your husband is not all-wise, all-knowing, and complete in himself, and if you've been guilty of hoodwinking him into thinking he is (because you believe that's what you're *supposed* to do), you haven't been dealing honestly with the love of your life. Conversely, if you've been trying to convince him that *you* are wiser. more capable, and more clever than he, you've leaned too far the other way. You may just fall in the lake and find that you're all wet. Your abilities are to complement his like a luscious apricot on a strong, upright tree.

Know Your Strengths

It is said that women, generally speaking, are detail people. That is an exciting thought! That's one reason why they make better mothers than men, among other things. Children need someone who pays attention to the little things that seem very big in their lives—like how to make a crayon behave itself on paper; the importance of keeping tiny fingernails clean; someone who listens to how they won at marbles; the fact that Bratso Billy threw sand in their eyes; and someone who will play "This Little Pig Went to Market" on their toes. When their toes are no longer tiny and have reached the big, eye-popping stage, they need to know that someone cares that the teacher was unfair today, and that the popular kids at school snub them. They need someone who will build them up when everything else is trying to tear them down. This is so important that even women who have no children of their own can fill this need in the lives of those who have no one else to care.

Your husband needs this God-given gift of yours as a detail person, even if he doesn't know he does. He needs your unique feminine cleverness. He needs your compassion and your strength. He needs you to help him become a man who carries out God's directives toward you and your family.

A woman who would rather let Husband continue his little-boy ways after he is an adult instead of realizing the potential of his masculinity in all its grown-up splendor, a lady who does nothing to help him care less for self and more for others, a lady who settles for shaky peace-at-any-cost, is taking the easy way out and someday may have to answer to God for it.

God intended you to be a helper to your husband, not a pacifier for his weaknesses.

A woman who understands that this is part of her calling as a wife can then confidently realize that her answering that call is the highest and truest love she can show her husband. Not only will he benefit in every way, but so will she, for she will find him supplying her needs beyond her wildest dreams and will in turn discover that it is a pleasure being submissive to him.

Submission—What It Is

We've seen what submission is *not*. It is not being a doormat—an empty-headed, silent creature who squeaks only when commanded. It is not allowing your husband to mistreat you. It is not encouraging your husband, by saying or doing nothing, to continue in selfish, spiritually immature ways at the expense of those around him. It is not silently complying with his every wish without attempting to discuss it with him should you feel he is not being reasonable or wise.

It *is* allowing and encouraging him to be a strong, guiding force in the family. It *is* taking definite steps to strengthen his leadership by helping him act wisely in the best interests of his children and you. It *is* respecting him by pleasantly allowing *him* to decide if you cannot agree on a matter, and abiding by his decision. It *is* respecting him by complying with his wishes if they aren't unusually harmful to the family unit or against God's laws. It *is* meeting his needs lovingly. (See Chapter 9 for more on submission.)

Heart Check

If you're feeling that your husband needs to learn a bit about submission and that you'd like to inform him right now, forget it. It's the wrong approach. He'd just back off and set up some impenetrable defense. Remember, in order to get someone to listen to you so you can help him, you must establish the right to be heard—the first step in our husband-grooming planning. Just turn the page.

3

STEP ONE—RECLAIM YOUR QUEENSHIP

How often have you heard, "A man's home is his castle?" The idea is that when a man is in his castle, he should be considered KING. I'm not against that at all. I love treating George so he feels like a king. But, if your honey is king, what does that make you? His *queen,* of course—not a chunk of old furniture he ignores, nor just a hot fire he only starts to warm *him* up, nor a pair of comfortable slippers that he discards when they get worn.

If he has been treating you like that, perhaps he isn't the only one at fault. Perhaps *you,* like many women, have abdicated your queenship.

One of the queenliest wives in history is recorded in the Holy Scriptures. This lady's husband was a *real* king. Queen Esther knew the value of being beautiful to her husband in every way. We're told that he loved her above all other women. Now that was saying something! Eastern kings had rooms full of concubines, chosen from among the loveliest virgins of the land. It behooved Queen Esther to remain the top one not only in his sight but in the estimation of everyone else with whom she came in contact. She was gracious. She was beautiful. She was wise. Had she been given to tears, anger, or loss of self-control in any way, at least in her husband-king's presence, she might very well have lost her head in more ways than one.

We might find it a bit mind-stretching to compare ourselves to Esther in any way. And yet, I know women in the humblest of circumstances who possess a regal queenliness about them.

You Don't Need Royal Blood

My grandmother was just such a lady. Having come from a family in the East which didn't know wealth, but knew what was "proper" and what was not, she carried the influences of her upbringing with her to the very wild West, where her new husband became a gold miner. When he was taken in death, she was left in a rough mountain town with her one child, my mother, and no knowledge of how to do anything but work in a post office (which she had done at home, where her father was the postmaster).

But since there was no post office available, the gold had run out, and she had a child to support, something had to be done. So she walked regally down the stairs of the hotel where they were staying and applied for the job of chambermaid! Each day she thoroughly cleaned each room, handling dirty laundry and flushing the hotel "toilets" by dumping buckets of water down the chutes that stretched to the earth below.

With just as much dignity later on, she opened her own laundry service for miners, carrying water some distance from a stream and scrubbing shirts and underclothes on a washboard, until every trace of grease and dirt was out of them. They were going to adorn nothing more than sweaty bodies bent on getting ore out of a stubborn earth, but she smoothed them to perfection with a very heavy iron that had to be heated on a stove top.

She kept her hair "just right," and her few clothes and those of her daughter were always neat and clean. She wasn't given to losing her self-control or complaining about her "bad luck."

When at last she was able to open a little post office in that mountain town, she had the respect of those who knew her. The frosting on the cake was that one of those handsome miners fell in love with her, even though he was 20 years younger than she was. They married and lived, very much in love, until she died at 84. Brokenhearted, he neglected his health and died two years later.

Assert Your Queenliness

When I was in college, a group of us was sent by our school to towns in the state where we would perform musically and dramatically for high school students, to encourage them to choose our halls of learning over others. One time several fellows were in the car in which my friend, Ruth, and I were riding. During the trip the boys became silly and a bit rowdy. They started pushing my head and doing some not-so-nice teasing. I didn't like it, but I laughed because I didn't want anybody to think I was a poor sport. Later, when we were alone, Ruth said, "I wouldn't ever let them treat *me* like that!"

Afterward I wondered, "How can you *not* let big guys treat you like that?" The secret she held was in her very demeanor. She was full of fun, but always poised, with a quiet, firm spirit that said, "You treat me with respect." I learned the lesson and from then on I *expected* the male gender to treat me respectfully. It paid off. Furthermore, I carried it into my marriage. I have never been able to accept less than top treatment from my husband. He's my knight in shining armor, my lover and my friend. I intend to help him stay that way.

Some years ago, when I would call him on the telephone, he would answer, occasionally, with a "Yes . . ." that sounded like, "I'm trying very hard to be polite but you are keeping me from doing something far more important than talking to you." You've had people do that to you when they answer the phone, haven't you? Doesn't it cause you to press your lips together and narrow your eyes? Perhaps it dissolves your daily portion of self-confidence in a flash. Maybe your voice even takes on a tinge of coldness in return. I realize that some people don't know they are sounding rude. They don't even *hear* themselves. But I still don't like it. So I had a talk with George about it, acting out what I was hearing and what I would prefer to hear. Now he sounds as if he's *glad* I'm calling. This may sound like a little thing, but it's important to me.

One time, not too long ago, George invited a single friend and his date to our home on a Sunday night to watch a TV movie about Jesus. It had been a crowded week and I could do little to prepare for Sunday evening until Sunday evening. So when the movie began I was still preparing the food, which I wanted to be special, since the friend he invited was a gourmet cook.

George said, "Come on, Honey. Sit down. It's starting." I did as he asked, but at commercial time, nervous about the food not being prepared, I slipped into the kitchen again. Each time the commercial was over he'd yell, "Come on! It's starting !"

Finally, during the commercial just before the final segment, I had nothing more to do besides arranging the refreshments attractively on the table which I had set up in the TV room. Even though the show had started again, I zipped quietly back and forth between the kitchen and the family room with various dishes, fussing over the food and keeping an eye on the TV at the same time. It never occurred to me that George wouldn't understand my dilemma. At various intervals he would say, "Sit down."

"All right," I would answer. "I've just a little more to do."

All of a sudden, with a loud, angry voice and a I'm-king-cut-off-your-head look on his face, he ordered, "I SAID SIT DOWN!"

I was humiliated. He had *never* spoken to me like that in front of anyone, and seldom when we were alone in the heat of disagreement. My face felt like fire. I was glad it was dark. I sat down, but I can't tell you what I saw. I was so crushed I couldn't concentrate on the movie.

I smiled as bravely as I could throughout the rest of the evening, when what I wanted to do was run to our bedroom and cry out my heart.

After the guests had gone home, I pulled out all the queenliness I could muster and told him what he had done to me. He couldn't *"iM-AAAgine"* what I had to be upset about. After all, he was doing it for my own good, wasn't he?

Until just recently, I dreaded having to face his friend, because the incident struck so deeply. There has been no hint of a repeat of my husband's performance since then, and he has promised me there never will be, even though he can't understand *yet* why it bothered me.

Jolene said, "When my husband used to *order* me to do something, I would turn quietly to him and assert, 'I'm not one of the children. If you want me to do something, I'll do it just as quickly if you ask me to, and I'll feel a whole lot better about you.' He seldom orders me around anymore."

When Georgia's Chuck starts putting her down or speaks angrily to her, she states calmly, "I'm a lady. When you decide to treat me like a lady, I'll be happy to talk with you," and quietly leaves the room.

It's letting your king know he's married to a queen, not an inferior person, and the practice of lopping off queens' heads is not in style anymore.

Above Cheapness

Nor would a queenly wife give an inch to any action that cheapened her. Ken had an irritating habit of poking at Lorraine's breasts and other intimate parts when he came home from work. After dodging him time and again, she finally asked, "Do you notice that whenever you come near me, I jump away? I can't enjoy snuggling up to you, or even sitting next to you, because you poke and push at me. There are two reasons why it bothers me, I think. First, it's natural for me, as a woman, to try to protect myself. And secondly, I don't like to be treated cheaply by the one I love!'' At last he understood, for she had asserted the fact of her queenliness, and it struck home.

Dorothy's Fred would do the same thing, only he was so rough that it hurt. Talking to him did no good. One day, as he came near, she beat him to it and grabbed at *his* intimate parts, squeezing hard.

Angrily he yelled, ''That hurt!''

''Now you know how it feels,'' she shot back. ''Maybe we can treat each other with more respect in the future.'' He never touched her in that manner again.

Losing Loveliness

Toileting in front of your husband is not queenliness. It is not attractive—not in sight or sound. Using dental floss while he's looking, making your mouth look like a cartoon caricature, does you no favors. Personal hygiene should be private, including anything to do with your monthly period. Slopping around in front of him very often in ill-fitting clothes in which you are embarrassed to be seen by the mailman is not very flattering to the love of your life. Reserving nice hairdos only for your trips to the grocery store or church and spending a good deal of your time around your husband in curlers and no makeup is not getting with it. Failing to wash yourself daily (make that several times a day during your menstrual period or illness), so as to avoid body odor, is an assault on his endurance.

Be Attractive On The Outside

A written question we received at a seminar

was, "How do you go about telling your wife that she doesn't look good?" Most men will not take a chance of offending their ladies by telling them they don't like their looks. If they have hinted at this they've been ignored, so they've given up.

There is so much written on this subject that you would think you would see fewer drabby wives around. I know that many women are that way because their husbands never compliment them, even when they're prettied up. They get discouraged and develop a feeling of "Why bother?" But my friend Suzy Willhite, who does much public speaking, retorts with, "Women should fix themselves up for themselves, if they don't have husbands who appreciate it! It makes them feel so much better, and they'll have much more confidence!" It's true.

One day while I was busy writing this book, a car drove into the driveway. My morning make-up had worn off, my hair had flown out of its combing from some garden work I had done for exercise, and I hadn't bothered to change out of my work clothes into something more attractive. I had thoughts in my mind I didn't want to lose, so I was making my typewriter clatter.

The driver of the car, a woman acquaintance of mine, saw me through the window. I was caught in all my disarray! After we had talked awhile, she looked at me suddenly and said, "Margaret, you look awfully tired."

"I do?" I returned.

She started her motor. "In fact, you look sick. I'm saying it in love, of course."

With that as her parting shot she was gone. When I went inside, I checked in the mirror. She was right. I looked tired. I looked sick.

But I was neither. I changed my clothes, redid my makeup and my hair, and rechecked the glassy truth-teller. The sick had gone. The tired had gone. And it drove home a valuable lesson to me. I should strive as often as possible never to look "sick and tired," especially when my husband is around. I don't always stick to that resolve, but I'm always glad when I do.

As you grow older, your beauty just isn't the same as it was when you were younger. You feel the same inside, but you don't look the same on the outside, and we might as well face up to that. Furthermore, we live in a youth-oriented society, which doesn't help matters one bit. A wise woman checks her beauty frequently and makes herself as presentable as possible.

It's stretching a man's imagination a bit far to expect him to tell you that you look prettywhen you don't. Many men don't even insist upon pretty wives. One man wrote, "It isn't important for her to look like Mrs. America. The important thing is that she is feminine and keeps herself looking *nice.*"

When You Dine Together

It isn't "putting on" to be a lady when you are out with your husband or at home. I'm often reminded of my mother, who is always a lady. Although my childhood was one of very humble circumstances, and my parents' lives were hard, we were expected to have good manners at every meal. In years to come, that teaching to be "proper" served me well in hundreds of circumstances. And yet, our table was always graced with her laughter and much conversation.

A woman who is a good conversationalist can

become fascinating to a man. Needless to say, discussion of depressing happenings should be avoided. It's very hard on the digestion and can turn a happy time into a quarrelsome or edgy session.

Chewing Your Cud?

During dinner, eat a bite and then relax for a few seconds while you chew it slowly, with your mouth closed, and before picking up your fork again. Only cows should chew continually with no break and their mouths open. After you swallow, take another bite, relax, chew slowly. Searching through your food with your fork, like you're inspecting it for bugs, is a no-no.

Keep your eyes full of interest, sympathy, laughter, or whatever suits the occasion as you focus most of your attention on your husband. Tell him how good-looking he is. Sit with a straight back. It's absolutely astounding what sparkling eyes and a big smile can do to turn a woman into romance bait!

All The Time

When you walk, walk tall, with your stomach in, your female pulchritude out, your head up, your chin in, and a pleasant and friendly manner reflected in your face. If you're the type to join your teenagers in a rough game of basketball, or you like to tumble on the floor with your little ones, by all means do it. If you have a funny bone that won't stop, laugh and laugh until your sides ache. A truly queenly person is neither a snob nor unapproachable, and a sense of humor and the ability to have fun is one of her greatest assets.

Pride Isn't All Bad

The daughter of the King of all kings shouldn't ever have to beg for her sustenance or help from other people or the government. Her Father has promised to take care of her. If her faith is tinier than that of a lettuce seed, she can still rely on that promise. The pride that comes from that knowledge is a healthy one. If you have a tendency to ask people for rides, or to babysit, or for other favors very often, when you don't reciprocate in some way, think it through carefully. Ask yourself, "Could I wait until I am able to do it myself? Is it necessary? Is there an alternate plan that I could handle independently of others?" You'll not only develop a good pride in the abilities that God has given you, but He will bless you for it. Furthermore, you will enjoy the respect of others and find out that life needn't be a constant mooch.

If you are one of the very few people whom the Father has ordained to be totally dependent on others because your physical abilities have been taken away, then there can be a pride in that as well. You are extremely special to be trusted with the responsibility of living like a princess in the light of such overwhelming burdens. He has allowed it, perhaps so that despite your trial you will shine forth His love and His glory to a frightened world.

Recently I had the joy of dealing with a young lady whose life was an encyclopedia of tragedies resulting from sin. She had given birth to an illegitimate child, had been ostracized by friends and family, and had experienced mental illness, rape, a stabbing, drugs, and about anything else you can name. But one day in my living room she threw herself on the floor, sobbing, and gave her life to Jesus.

In the ensuing months she learned many valuable lessons as she took her first wobbly steps of faith. And one of them was a healthy pride in caring for herself and her child, without reaching her hand out to others. There were many testings, but she stayed on course. Among other testings, she lost her job, but she trusted God to supply. "God will bring it in," she would tell people. "I know He will." And He did.

Be Somebody

We had just finished speaking to a congregation made up almost entirely of people of practically every ethnic background, who had low income and little education. A slim woman, tiny in stature, made her way up to me. Dignity, warmth, and intelligence were written on her wrinkled but attractive black face, even though she looked most distressed.

She had reared five children. Now that they were grown she wanted to go to college. Her husband had said no. She wanted to sew clothes for herself, now that she no longer had to sew for the children, but he said no. He wanted her to simply wait on him and be available, which left her with a lot of free hours on her hands. Arthritis had begun to take its toll on her body, and she wanted to utilize what little time she had left.

The story wasn't new to me. Women who have subjugated their own personalities and desires to care entirely for others most of their lives, with no chance to pursue any of their own interests, often have a longing in their hearts to find out if they are individuals or just an extension of somebody else.

If you are at that point in your life, you may have to make a change of some sort. Don't get me wrong. There is no higher calling in life than that of a wife and mother. I firmly believe that. A woman who shoves her loved ones' needs aside to look for what she thinks is going to be a sunnier climate too often finds rain instead. But time can be carved out of your schedule to pursue activities that you enjoy and that will benefit not only you but also the family. Maybe you'll want to sell a little real estate on the side, or take a correspondence course in Greek.

If your husband is a "no" person, you might be surprised at his reaction if you go ahead and do it before you mention it to him. Many women told me in my survey that their husbands say very little once it's done. They may fuss about it for awhile in some instances, but they seem to be relieved that they aren't being called upon to make the decision. Of course, if your husband has already said no to something, there's no sense in pursuing it. That would just cause unhappiness between you. He may change his mind about it further down the line.

If you can include him in some way, all the better. Turn him into a cheering squad, as Delia did. She kept Bill feeling good by asking his opinions regarding her limited venture into politics and by following his advice as often as possible.

Or be like Connie, who, after 20 years of marriage, started singing publicly. From the beginning she told Phil, "I need you there to critique my performance." Later, when they could afford sound equipment, he took over the operating of it, which he enjoyed very much.

Caution

I'm not talking about becoming a different person! A friend of mine told me that she had always wanted her husband to be more romantic and attentive. But it seemed that nothing worked. So one day she decided she'd try all the little methods described in a magazine article about how to keep her husband fascinated. After she tried this cute trick and that, her husband told her he wanted to have a talk. Since he seldom initiated talking with her, it worried her considerably. When they were alone he told her she had changed, and he didn't like it. He went on to say that if she didn't become herself again, the one he fell in love with, he was leaving.

Being the real you, in your best sense, is essential. Baseness, crudeness, dullness, laziness, mousiness, bullishness, and other negatives are what we're trying to avoid. A happy, energetic approach to life, poise, a sense of self-worth, a *knowing* that you deserve respect and taking steps to assure that you get it in a loving way—*this* is what we are trying to achieve.

Heart Check

If you're thinking a bit unkindly about yur sweetie because he's been all king with no queen, clamp your lips shut with some clothespins, if necessary, until those emotions subside. Stay lovely. Then you'll have more confidence to tackle the next step in showing real love to your man.

4

STEP TWO—DEFINE YOUR PROBLEM

◆────────────────────────────────

Whatever the area of most concern to you, whether it be that of communication, sexual relations, romance, help around the home, money, children, or relatives, you want a dream man who will understand your needs and respond with positive action. To reach your golden goal you must define your problem.

Hers Was Huge!

If choosing a starting place seems a bit ponderous to you, be glad you aren't faced with a decision as weighty as the one Queen Esther had. We admired her in Chapter 3. We'll sympathize with her now, for she had a concern that was not only unavoidably major, but it needed tending to immediately.

The decision had been handed to her by the uncle who had reared her in place of her parents, who were not living. Her husband, King Ahasuerus, had made a very big decision that simply had to be reversed, for many thousands of lives depended upon it— the lives of Queen Esther's own people, the Jews.

It seems that this powerful king, who ruled over 127 provinces from India to Ethiopia and was greatly feared, pulled a boo-boo by listening with half an ear to his powerful right-hand man, Haman, who asked him for permission to slaughter all the Jews in the land. Haman told the king that the Jews were ignoring the esteemed ruler's laws and commands. Naturally, in kingly style, Ahasuerus didn't like that. In fact, it made him furious—so much so that he gave Haman the okay to go ahead with wiping them all out.

What the monarch didn't know was that Haman wasn't telling him the truth. The truth was that Haman was miffed because *one* Jew, Mordecai, ignored *Haman's* command to bow down to him when he passed by. Had he realized that Mordecai was the queen's own uncle, he might have gone about getting his revenge a bit differently. But he didn't realize this, and soon word blasted out of the palace that a day had been set for the carnage.

Naturally, Mordecai became more than a little upset. In panic, he sent word to Esther that she had better do something about it.

His request put her in a terrible quandary! She couldn't just run to the king and cry on his shoulder, because no one, but *no* one, neither man nor woman, was allowed to go near the king if the king hadn't called him or her. To do so could mean sudden death, and Esther hadn't been summoned by her husband for 30 days.

Nervously she sent this bit of information to her uncle. Mordecai shot back that if she didn't do something anyway, God would take care of it by sending help from someone else. (Although God is not mentioned in the account—His sovereignty is implied.) Furthermore, Mordecai warned Esther that she herself would not escape, because all in the palace would be destroyed. He capped it off with this gem: "Who knows but what you were put in

the position of queen for this very purpose?''
(My paraphrase.)

That struck home. With no time to waste, she
delivered her famous observation, ''. . . if I
perish, I perish,'' and laid some very careful
groundwork. We'll pick up the threads of
Esther's dramatic dilemma later on, but
meanwhile. . . .

Concerning You

Your challenge may seem miniscule in comparison to Queen Esther's, and it's unlikely that
your problem is compounded by the possibility
of your head being literally chopped off should
you approach your husband with it. Never-
theless, it is important to you, and therefore the
solution to it is worth planning carefully.

If you've read many books or attended
seminars on how to improve your life, you
were probably told to make a list. As a result,
you may be listed almost to death! I think lists
are very useful, but for our purposes let's use a
more creative approach, so that this entire project can be fun from beginning to end. How
about . . .

. . . cutting out pictures of men (from
magazines or newspapers) doing what you
would like to see your's doing to supply
your needs and pasting them in a *secret*
scrapbook entitled ''A Beautiful Picture of
My Husband'' (colorfully printed on the
first page). Then, on the back page, you can
write the defining statement ''. . .
someday.'' Or,

. . . drawing pictures of same. Or,

. . . writing down dream-husband items on different-colored paper strips, rolling them up and dropping them into jars decorated by you—one jar for each category of dream. Or,

. . . writing them on smaller pieces, laying them in a music box so you can take one out to the accompaniment of happy sounds when the time is right.

Those are but a sample. You'll think of even better ways to enjoy your undertaking. As you put each part of your dream man in a jar or scrapbook, consider every item carefully. Maybe what you *think* you want or *say* you want in a husband isn't what you *really* want at all!

Your Real Desires

One time we were speaking in Nebraska when I met the nicest little husband! He was not the happiest little husband I've met. I found out the reason as he shared with me. It seems that his wife had always complained that he could never make a decision. He was wishy-washy and namby-pamby in her estimation. He just wouldn't take leadership in the home, she declared, and how she *longed* to have him do so. For 32 years she had hammered at him and expressed her displeasure over his weakness. Well, a man can take just so much! It was time, he decided, to start being head of the household.

The opportunity to try his newfound masculinity came shortly after his momentous decision. His wife entered the room authoritatively and spread some travel folders on the table.

"We're taking a vacation, Melvin. See? We're going to sail on this ship to Tahiti." As she warmed up to her subject, he was trying to still his wildly beating heart so that when his words popped out, they wouldn't squeak.

When she finished speaking, he drew himself up to his full height of 5'4" and announced, "We're not going."

"What?" she responded incredulously. "Why not?"

"It's too expensive. I have other plans for us." (Well, anyway, he was in the process of thinking about starting to make other plans.) "And as head of this house, I've decided that we're not going."

Her eyes bugged out, she drew herself up higher than his 5'4", and returned, "Well! You may not be going, but I am!" And she did. That's why he was attending our lecture on marriage by himself.

You see, that woman had been talking just to hear her head rattle all those years. She was trying to impress him and others with the fact that she was all the right things a wife should be, and he was all the wrong things a husband shouldn't be. But she had no desire or intention of ever letting that little man be head of their home.

Examine your true desires. Ask yourself, "If this particular situation changed, and he did what I am asking, would it be what I *really* want?" If you say, for instance, that you wish your husband would fix things in the house when they break down, would you feel a real sense of loss if he started doing them and you could no longer complain to him or others that he just doesn't have what it takes? Some women derive a feeling of superiority by believing that their husbands are not capable in certain areas.

An example is one alcoholic's wife who let the world know how much she hated his alcoholism, and yet she was so threatened by his new found strength when he became cured that she got a divorce.

Terry was one who got what she wanted and then wished she didn't have it. She learned the hard way that her husband's reluctance to allow her to make decisions in the money market was well-founded. Eventually, he gave in to her urging, handing all their family economic affairs over to her. She nearly had a nervous breakdown. She couldn't handle it. She begged him to take the job back, and she had a greater appreciation of his abilities in that area from then on.

Have you found something you should eliminate? All right. Now, ask yourself,

What Can I Do For Myself?

Women are amazingly capable people. They can accomplish almost anything they set their minds to do. If you can pick up your drooping chin, soften your tense lips, put a smile on your face, and place in your heart the knowledge that you are super able, then you can take care of some of your needs yourself, at least temporarily.

Tina had tried to get Jim to fix the bathtub for months. Finally she stopped in a hardware store, asked a few questions, and purchased some white gooey stuff which she took home. Her husband said. "Yeah. That'll do it. I'll get to it soon." But he didn't. So Tina read the directions and found that it was not difficult at all to squeeze the miracle product around the edges of the tub herself! The problem was solved.

Calling Upon Others

After you've decided what you can do for yourself, check the jar or scrapbook contents again. Ask, "What needs have I that other people besides my husband could supply without it being a threat to him or our relationship?" (It goes without saying that you'll want to be very careful not to become a pest to anyone else.)

Sylvia wanted her kitchen papered. Tad wouldn't help her. By casting about, she discovered a friend of hers who wanted to paper her den. They decided to join forces and help each other!

If you start taking care of some of your needs by tending to them yourself or calling upon others, you'll find it easier to tackle what's left of those items carefully pictured in your scrapbook, and you won't be quite so apt to approach that mister of yours in an emotional, self-pitying way, for the load will be lighter and you will have gained confidence. Consider something else:

Is It Really Worth Fussing About?

A lot of ladies spend a lot of time being concerned about a lot of things that aren't all that important.

My husband has precious little time to spend

in doing garden and yard chores, so on Saturdays, if he isn't traveling to lecture, he whirls through the yard as an absolute terror to weeds, bugs, and sometimes perfectly innocent and faithful little plants.

Once the sun is up, it is generally too late for me to make any suggestions regarding the part of the garden that is receiving his blessings.

Last spring we decided we would put in a fairly good-sized vegetable garden, and I was assigned the organizing and overseeing of the planting which the young people were to do. George happened to be standing by when I commented, "The cucumbers need sandy soil."

"No," he pronounced. "I'm not bringing in anything more than what is right there. Let's get them planted. They'll do just fine."

His tone of voice was final. He was a man *on his way,* and he couldn't be bothered with unimportant things like what the plants wanted. They'd like what they got or lump it.

I had tried to plant cucumbers before, and discovered that they seldom lump it. Two weeks later, though, when we were in the garden, and I was feeling sorry for them, I muttered as I watered them, "You poor little things need sand so you can breathe, don't you?"

George heard me, took a look at them gasping for breath, and happily agreed, "Better get some."

As it turned out, when I added sand, it was too late for some of the plants. Half the cucumbers succumbed, but the other half forgave the primary insult and continued to grow, gaining in strength and at last producing some nice future pickles.

Had I stood up to my husband initially, perhaps bringing on an argument, or allowing the young people to see me undermine his leadership a little in front of them, I might have had a few more cucumbers, but a little cloud could have come between us.

Turning Negatives Into Positives

If you've decided that your motives are as pure as new-driven snow; if you've determined you *can* do some things for yourself; if you've discovered that calling upon others can be rewarding; and if you've come to the conclusion that some irritations just aren't worth fussing about, then you can move ahead another notch by casting an analytical eye at his exasperating habits to see if perhaps a potential strength is lurking there.

A classic example of a wife unearthing such potential was provided by a lady with whom I counseled who said that her husband continually dominated conversations, not only with her, but with everyone else. He *loved* what he had to say! He also loved people, and conversing was the joy of his life. Before he became a Christian and gave up drink, it was even worse. One glass and he was off and running—running others right out of the party.

She didn't feel she could say, "You know, you're a big bore!" It would have hurt his feelings and perhaps would have destroyed the very quality in him that could make him a success later on. But she was determined not to let it rest for 20 years, either. She used the positive approach and said, "You know, Honey, you have such a superb way of putting words together to form ideas. Maybe someday you'll become a writer, or a public speaker—possibly a salesman.''

He was flattered, of course, and while he was mulling over those possibilities she let loose with the coup de grace. "Since you enjoy being with people so much, it would probably be a good idea to jot down some of the thoughts and ideas you pick up from listening to them. You could keep them in a file and someday they might be of use.'' She said no more, but committed it to prayer. Her loving cleverness brought about two positive results: he stopped talking so much so he could listen to ideas to jot down for his files; and he started writing, which led him to a career in public speaking.

Or you can consider leaving a husband's disturbing trait as is and using it to your own advantage. My husband's tendency to work longer hours so we eat very late is a plus for me. It gives me extra time to pursue my own interests, such as music, drama, and writing.

Listen To Grandma

The older generation has a lot of wisdom if we'd just stop for a few minutes to listen. We've become so youth-oriented in this country that aged mothers and grandmothers are shoved in the corner as if they're some sort of dolts who lost all their intelligence as soon as *we* reached maturity.

One older person whom I interviewed for this book, an aunt of my husband's, is now married to her fourth husband. They tied the knot after she was in her eighties. All the former husbands had passed away. I said, "Aunt Adele, tell me about your first husband."

She smiled dreamily. "He was the father of my children. He was a wonderful man!"

"And the second?"

"Oh, he was a wonderful man."

"The third?"

"He was a wonderful man, too."

"And the present? No, don't tell me. I think I know. He's a wonderful man."

We both laughed and she continued. "Yes, all my husbands were wonderful. They all had their good points. I tried to dwell on those."

I watched her during the meal. She and I were talking, but she kept one ear open to what our two husbands were discussing, and every now and then she'd glance at her mate and smile sweetly, nodding her head as if to say, "Yes, that's right. You are so wise."

She said she always let each husband be head of the family. I asked, "Did you ever stand up for your rights?"

"Oh, yes, if I felt it was important. I would stand firm. But if he became angry, I would back off, wait and come in later from a different angle. There's always a better way. None of my husbands ever failed to do anything I asked, eventually."

"Did you criticize them?"

"Why should I criticize? They were doing their best. I helped them do better sometimes."

Back To The Scrapbook

Now that you have eliminated, at least temporarily, some of the gripes you had when you started, and you have given every benefit of the doubt where potential is concerned, it's time to get started on those traits of his that really should go. But you'll have to remind yourself of the old axiom, "Inch by inch life's a cinch, but yard by yard life is hard." He will be more willing to comply with your desires if you guide him up and over a hill rather than a rugged mountain, at least at first.

Likewise, if you race headlong into a difficulty that you and he have wrangled much over, one which raises his hackles immediately, you may not reach the finish line.

So out of all those prettied-up goodies, choose only one with which you intend to work, and one of minor importance for now. After a time, as you show him that doing *for* you is not only painless, but that it makes him a happier, more contented, very masculine man, and that it makes you a happier, more contented, very feminine woman, you can get back to the more serious difficulties.

Heart Check

If you've faced up to some wrong attitudes on your part, take concrete action now to correct yourself, before you go any farther in helping your honey change. If you check out A-1, move on to the next step.

5

STEP THREE— SPELL IT OUT
WITH WORDS

Basic to all solutions to husband-wife togetherness is proper communication, which includes that done with the eyebrows, other facial expressions, body language, writing, and reactions to stimuli. It also encompasses talking and spelling it out with action. We'll concentrate on the last two—talking and action.

Remember the old comic strip "Maggie and Jiggs"? Maggie got her points across to Jiggs by yelling, clunking him on his bald pate with a rolling pin, or whirling him through the air until she could deposit him against a wall. Although you might wish you could resort to such methods at times, there are better ways.

Hear The Men

Since I often whip out surveys of various sizes to get the pulse of public thinking on an issue, I did so this time by asking a number of men what female reactions most effectively moved them to do as their wives wanted. Except for one who said "Never!" and several who said "Sometimes," all the men felt the best way was for wives to tell them frankly how they feel.

Most certainly letting him know straight out is the *first* attempt you should make to help your man understand how important it is to you that he deal with any particular problem in a way that will satisfy that hurting down inside. Honest, open communication is the advice that comes from many successfully married couples.

George and I let each other know how we feel about nearly everything, and we've done so since before we said we'd stick together for life. One of the reasons why he has a listening ear is that, as a lawyer, he has dealt with so many people in divorce cases who managed to have a number of children, but couldn't talk to each other. He says that one husband, who was suing for divorce, but who hadn't retained his own attorney yet, looked at his wife incredulously as, in the safety of my husband's office, she spilled out the feelings she had bottled up inside for years. At last he blurted, "Why haven't you told me you felt like this? I had no idea!" It was to late for her, because he already had another woman by then, but it pointed out again to us that some people just don't let each other know.

On The Other Hand

"I've TRIED it, again and again!" Corrinne wailed to me. Dozens of voices echoed through my memory as I recalled others who say that husbands aren't hearing what frustrated wives are saying! One can't converse with another person who refuses to talk or who turns off his listening apparatus.

If that sounds unhappily familiar to you, it's time to open up new ways of communication, so that you and your love can start being *one* again. As carefully as an attorney must prepare his case for presentation in court, you must pave your way. My husband says, "Women have amazing power with men when they use their coquettish ways with them." Whether co-quettish or not, one of the first things to do is . . .

Choose The Right Time
To Get His Attention

Even in the best relationships, there are moments when it isn't advisable to bulldoze your way into a person's RIGHT NOW and lay your bill of rights on his thinking. There are moments when a man's tolerance level, especially when it comes to problems, is very low.

Dr. Keith Fleshman, a former schoolmate of mine and a missionary doctor, wrote, "One problem is the full-sponge syndrome, last-straw syndrome, I've-had-it-up-to-here syndrome. The professional contact heaps problems on until you just have to go home, crawl in a corner, and hide. Meantime, the wife has absorbed all she can bear of . . . problems, insubordination (from children) . . . or whatever burdens . . . so she unburdens and gets rejected. . . ."

Let's own up to it. There are moments when *you* would rather not have to talk with anyone, right? Since husbands are usually home when everyone else is, it isn't awfully difficult to understand why they might need time to themselves. But after he's had some breathing space, go ahead with your plan.

Get His Attention In The Right Way

You recall reading in Chapter 4 that Queen

Esther made the statement, "If I perish, I perish." Her knees had taken to shaking because there was no way she could get to her husband, the king, without inviting herself into his throne room.

Knowing that she was a beautiful woman, loved by the king above all others, didn't reassure Esther too much either. The reason she became queen in the first place was because her predecessor, Vashti, had dared to defy one of the king's orders. She lost her queenship and who knows what else. The Bible doesn't go into those gory details. Being married to Ahasuerus was like being written on a blackboard. You never knew when you'd be erased.

But since some people she loved would soon be murdered, possibly including herself, Esther had to get her husband's attention somehow, and hopefully in such a manner that she wouldn't lose her pretty head before she had a chance to present her desperate petition.

So she made her move. First, she led all the Jews of the land and the young women who waited on her hand and foot in a three-day fast. This meant that neither she nor they ate or drank, and, although it is not mentioned in the account, they probably also prayed, for traditionally fasting and prayer went hand-in-hand.

Secondly, on the fateful day, not knowing if she would live to see another day, Esther dressed in her royal robes. In doing so, she would be reminding her king that she wasn't just another woman in his harem. She was his queen. By dressing the part, she felt the part. Her very demeanor would command respect.

The walk to the court which lay just outside

the throne room, where the king took care of matters of state, must have seemed far too short to Esther. Trying to ignore her quivery insides, she glided into position— JUST—into the king's view should he look up. Television beauties could never compete. She stood there quietly, stately, and gorgeous . . . waiting.

When Ahasuerus raised his head for a moment he caught sight of his lady. His stomach did a quick turnover, and his heart leaped within him. Can't you almost hear his thoughts? *Esther! She knows the rules. Wasn't she prepared for a year before she was chosen as my wife? Why then is she here?*

The king was no fool, though. He knew Esther wouldn't have risked her life unless she had something very important to discuss with him. Thus the king who was smitten with love didn't *just* raise his golden scepter. As soon as his beauty had walked forward with his permission, he asked, "What would you like, Queen Esther? And what is your request? It shall be given you up to half the kingdom."

Wise woman, Esther. Although she was burning inside, she didn't point at the man by the king's side and cry out, "That man has planned to murder all my people and me! Stop him!" Such an action would have been most embarrassing to the king. After all, he was the one who had chosen Haman to be second-in-command. Nor did Esther accept the offer of half the kingdom. Instead, keeping lovely control, she merely graciously invited the king—and the murderer—to a banquet. That rascal, Haman, never suspected that clever Esther was laying a trap for him.

And You?

If you aren't convinced about the wisdom of biding your time before spewing your gripes all over your Tarzan the minute he ventures inside the house, and would rather leave it to the threatened queens, hear an ancient proverb:

> A FOOL UTTERETH ALL HIS MIND
> BUT A WISE MAN KEEPETH
> IT IN TILL AFTERWARDS.

A wise woman also keeps it in until afterwards. Greet your man with a beautiful you, a clean house, and happy, clean children. (One husband told me, "When she has the kids lined up to meet me, it makes me feel *so* good!")

Of course, you will have his favorite meal wafting its yummy smells through the house, so he knows you *really* care about his most urgent urges. Most of my survey men tell me that softening them up with affection, cooking their favorite dishes, and showering them with niceties usually works to make them very receptive to their wives' requests.

You might even suggest by the way you are dressed, coupled with candles and flowers on the table, that you are looking forward to "making whoopee" that evening, which usually puts red-blooded males in a receptive mood.

Although some men resent being questioned about their day, most men like it, so after he's had a chance to breathe, make him feel important by showing interest in what happened to him since you saw him last.

After He's Eaten

Then, when a quiet moment comes up, you can smile into his eyes and say, "Sweetheart, do you think you could spare a half-hour for me sometime this evening? I need your input on something. I could be free as soon as the dishes are done, or when the children are in bed. Which would be best for you?"

Thus you've done three things so as not to scare him away.

1) You've said you *need his input,* thereby appealing to his ego;

2) You've given him some idea of *how long* it will take, so he isn't worried about you blowing his evening (stick to the agreed time if at all possible);

3) You've given him the choice of two *whens* so he can plan his time.

However you say it, try including those three ingredients. If dinner doesn't lend itself to suggesting a rendezvous in soft willowy tones, because the table is graced with small children who are spilling milk, talking loudly, or demanding attention when they head for the living room carpet with gooey vegetables decorating their fronts, wait until later, when everything has calmed down. For instance,

When He's Relaxed

How long has it been since you volunteered to plop down on your husband's lap? If he isn't given to a sense of humor, it might be in your best interest to consider another approach. Whether on his lap or off, slip your arm around his shoulder, smooth his cheek with your fingers, and kiss him on the corner of his lips. Before he has a chance to jump to conclusions and trundle you off to bed, say, "Sweetheart, I need your attention. I have to discuss something with you. It'll take about an hour. When would be a good time?" Most men can't resist *that*.

Suggest The Right Place

A French lop (rabbit to me) prepares her nest by pulling whisper-soft fur from under her chin so that when her newborn tumble out of their former secure existence into a new life, they are greeted with a delightful, comforting, warm welcome. If you wish to have super communication with your husband, you might learn from her example.

Once he agrees to a conference, you want to be ready with a suggestion of *where* you should get together, always without the children, for you need his full attention and he needs yours. See if some of the following are to your liking:

. . . If he loves the out-of-doors, share while you take evening walks together.

. . . Go out to dinner, if he enjoys that. Talk there and also afterwards, while driving home.

. . . Escape to your car, where you can discuss in peace.

. . . . At night when lying in bed together is a favorite spot for some people. One woman whose husband found it very difficult to share tried this with success, but she had to start with the lights out at first. Now they can talk with the lights on. If yours falls asleep . . . well, try something else.

. . . Before dinner, after he's had a glass of juice, sit on the floor, leaning against the bed, hold hands, and share.

. . . Schedule a little picnic together (no children, remember—you can make it up to them later).

. . . Sit before a roaring fireplace, leaning against pillows piled on the floor.

. . . Choose a couch where you can cuddle.

. . . Tell him what's on your mind while you give him a backrub.

. . . If he works in an office, meet him there. A pastor wrote, "My wife makes an appointment with me. That way I can't put it off and there are no distractions."

. . . If his mind tends to wander, choose as your place for discussion a small, plain room where he can't be as easily distracted.

See? A little imagination turns what could be an unpleasant situation into just the opposite. You'll find, as you start incorporating these ideas into your partnership, that you and he will begin looking forward to the times, even if some negative things have to be discussed.

Non-Talkers

If you have extremely poor or virtually *no* communication between you, forget the problems and the list (see Chapter 4) until you rebuild bridges. Your first effort, using the same techniques as mentioned, will be to discuss happy, nonthreatening subjects, drawing him out very slowly.

One fellow told me that he just couldn't converse with his wife. He said, "It's always been like that. I just freeze up when I think I should say something nice. I can't even discuss problems with her. I keep it all inside."

I pointed out to him that he was doing a pretty adequate job of talking with me in front of a whole group of men. So that meant that he *could* talk with his wife if he really *wanted* to. But once again, even though we needed to get at the root of the problem, it was probably wise to apply a Band-Aid to stop some of the bleeding. I suggested that he try speaking into a tape recorder when he was all alone, and have her play it back when he wasn't around. Or write notes and letters to her. He couldn't write, he felt, but he thought he might be able to tackle the machine. Your husband might be open to a similar suggestion. If *you* are the fly in the pancake mix and just can't say things out loud, use the foregoing suggestions yourself.

Look Beneath The Surface

You may have to analyze Mr. Handsome's background to discover the whys of his not talking. At a couples' retreat where George and I were speaking once, we had sent each couple to find a private spot where they could converse according to a blueprint we sent along with them. Before ten minutes had passed, a couple made their way toward me. Tears were simulating two swimming pool in the eyes of the very pretty wife, as she avoided looking at her good-looking husband, whose jaw was set like a chunk of granite. It was soon apparent that he wasn't talking to her or me, so she opened up.

Trying to keep her voice under control, she said, "You sent us out to talk over our problems. Our main problem is that he won't talk over our problems!" She was frustrated because she needed his input on family decisions.

As soon as he realized that I wasn't going to condemn him and was holding her as much responsible for the difficulty as he was, he began to answer my questions. I soon found out that the source of his reluctance was a common one among nontalkers. His parents seldom conversed, with each other or their children. Knowing the root cause wasn't enough for a solution, but the solution wasn't far behind. He revealed that what irritated him most was her tendency to burst into his thoughts.

"I know she needs to talk," he said. "But when I'm reading, or working on something, I resent her intrusion."

I asked him what *he* thought might be a solution, and gradually we came up with some possibilities that he was willing to try. Principally, he agreed to plan each week ahead, as much as possible, and set aside times when he would be available to her. In preparation for those times, he would plan nothing else, and would prepare his mind so that he would be receptive. In turn, she would not intrude upon the time he felt he needed alone, and would let him instigate most communication except during their appointed time together, when she could feel free to spill her thoughts to him.

The next day, after the retreat had ended, we were guest speakers at the host church which that couple attended. After the service they came rushing up to me with two of the handsomest little boys you ever saw. The eyes of the parents were sparkling and there was a happy energy that pulsated from them. He said, "It's working . . . beautifully! We're so excited! It's going to be terrific."

Heart Check

Patience, lovely one. If your first, second, and third attempts at queenly-type communication weren't too productive, that doesn't mean that the next attempt won't be, if you are willing to bide your time. You also may need to use other methods for a breakthrough. Keep on reading. There's more to the Queen Esther saga.

6

CONVERSE WITH WISDOM

Once you've got your husband's undivided attention, proceed in a wise, mature fashion. If you want to take a look at some ladies whose husbands have written to me, complaining about their wives' communication skills, here you are:

Betsy overreacts to any negatives her husband lets her know about. He has avoided sharing much with her because she panics, becomes fearful, and chews on it for weeks afterward. If he tells her about joyful happenings, she jumps on him as if she were going to ride him in the Kentucky Derby. It's safer for him to talk with someone else.

Helen loves to bring up the same subject again and again. She hashes over each detail to where Jack feels like he's listening to a scratched record that he can't take off the turntable.

Gladys always has her knitting clicking away when her husband is trying to discuss with her. She looks bored, and occasionally, in the middle of an important point he is making, she'll make some inane and irrelevent remark like, "Is that a zit on your face?" Her husband would like to see the knitting set aside and some sparkling, interested eyes looking at him.

Sue, a cautious creature by nature, puts all of Tom's ideas down with "It won't work;" "I don't agree;" "That's a dumb idea;" or similar creativity squashers. Or if she says nothing, she LOOKS squashy with a downturned mouth and a questioning eyebrow. Tom finally gave up. He found someone who thinks his ideas are great, though—one of the secretaries at work who doesn't have a husband.

Lana loves to remind her gentleman of his past mistakes in judgment. Todd is getting to where he doesn't like her very much.

Doris was born knowing EVERYTHING! As a result, whenever her hubby attempts to share his thoughts with her, she not only interrupts him continually, but she has advice and an answer to everything—on the spot — without batting an eyelash of thought. As Tory says, "Sometimes I'm telling her something just so I can get a better perspective on it. I can often come to my own conclusions that way, if she'll just give me half a chance."

Jackie can't resist correcting her husband's grammar continually when they are trying to converse, and if he repeats himself, she lets him know she's heard that before.

Patty has lots of things about her husband she wants changed, and she expects him to take her criticisms manfully. But when the tree turns a different color, and drops leaves in HER basket, she dissolves in tears or slams off in anger. Or she argues until she bullies him into admitting that his criticism is not justified.

Theresa feels that her husband doesn't love her if he doesn't agree with her thinking. So many sessions of communication have ended up with her feelings getting hurt that Dan mentally tiptoes around her, afraid to say what's on his mind.

Jenny insists on its being one way or not at all—hers. To compromise what SHE thinks is right is not in her experience. If she were willing to listen to Harold more, she'd find that he isn't exactly an idiot, and that some of his solutions might even be better than her own. She hasn't learned that demanding throws up walls. Once the wall is up, pride won't let her husband supply her needs.

Cretia has formed a habit of saying, "You NEVER . . ." (take me out, listen to me, etc.) or "You ALWAYS . . ." (are mean to me, too strict with the children, etc.). Since her short memory doesn't give him credit for the times he does do things right, Ronnie becomes discouraged and doesn't want to try at all.

Doxie has her every hour filled so much with children, pets, housework, and activities that about the only time Roy sees her alone is just before he can't keep his eyes open a minute longer at night. He feels that *everything* is more important to her than he is, so he has simply withdrawn into a conversational shell. When she rushes in with some hurried conversation, he isn't even slightly interested.

If you've just seen a prototype of yourself in

the preceding illustrations, you'll want to set about changing those hindrances to communication with a RUSH order.

If you go into your talking session together with a smile on your face and a warmth in your heart, and keep it there, no matter what transpires, your husband will be much more receptive.

Back At The Palace

In picking up the threads of the Queen Esther story, we find that her banquet was a huge success. She made it so delicious, so relaxing, so colorful, and so attractive to her V.I.P. husband that once again he offered half of his kingdom to her and asked her to tell him what was going on in her beautiful head. I don't know why she didn't tell him right then. Maybe she got cold feet. After all, when she revealed the facts, it would be either Haman's life or hers. So she demurred a second time. She refused to tell. She invited her king and the murderer to a second banquet instead, to be staged the following evening.

By this time, you can well imagine, she had a most curious, intrigued husband on her hands. So after her second evening of success, and a *third*-time offer of half the kingdom from her adoring man, she spoke boldly and straightforwardly, telling it just like it was.

Whew! Electricity thundered through the room and right to the outside, where the king went in his anger to calm himself and to think properly.

By this time Haman was in a panic! He would

have run, but where could he go? There was only one thing to do. He threw himself on the couch where Esther was sitting and began pleading for his life. Just his luck—at that very moment the king stalked back in. He was still angry, and seeing Haman trying to be persuasive with his wife didn't make him any less so. He shouted, "Will he also force the queen before me in the house?"

That was it. Dirty Haman was doomed and hanged on the very gallows he had ordered constructed for the neck-breaking of Mordecai, Esther's uncle. And all of this happened because Esther communicated to her husband in the right way.

What About You?

You have chosen one important subject, an item from your list. Resist the temptation to add other gripes, even if your husband is especially receptive. Only people who have excellent communication should attempt to air everything in one session. Besides the fact that socking it to him all at once might cause him to stalk away, never to get caught in your web again, it's a real fact that husbands who hear too much at one time simply can't remember it all. It's better to achieve success on one item and see it become a solid change than to watch him make a half-hearted attempt or no attempt at all on ten items.

Compliments Come First

Everyone, including you, likes to hear something nice about himself or herself. It's as welcome as a refreshing swim in 100-degree heat. You'll always get a better response if you let the person recognize the efforts he has made. So tell your husband a few things about him that are good and pleasing to you, especially as they relate to the subject you wish to discuss, either before you bring it up or as you relate it.

Clara couldn't get her husband to wear a shirt in the summertime when they had guests for dinner. He wore, instead, a white undershirt. He didn't believe in "putting on the dog," and they had many a wrangle over it, with Clara ending up as embarrassed as ever and her husband more stubborn than ever. This was characteristic of much of their marriage, in fact, and eventually they divorced.

If Clara had communicated differently, she might have seen a different reaction. Like Mildred. Mildred's problem wasn't an undershirt. It was a tie. Her husband wouldn't wear a tie, even to go to church. Since they hadn't seen eye-to-eye on this for some time, when she began her talking sessions with her husband, she avoided that subject altogether.

Finally, after they'd had eight successful "talks" at different times, about other subjects, she decided it was time to try again. the conversation went something like this:

"I want to thank you for helping me so many times when I've needed it. You've been wonderful in these little conferences we've had."

"I've kind of enjoyed them myself."

Giving him a hug and a kiss, she continued, "I love you so much. You're such a terrific husband."

"It must be a big one this time."

"It really isn't. It's just big to me, because . . . well, I guess I have weaknesses in some areas. And maybe, since you're so much stronger, and can do things that you don't even want to do without it hurting you, you'd do something just for me—because you love me, with all my silliness."

"Maybe. What is it?"

"It's all wrapped around the fact that I think you're so handsome, and I'm so proud of you when we're out. I want to show you off to your best advantage."

"Okay, Honey, get on with it."

She put her head on his shoulder. "Promise you won't be mad at me? I couldn't stand that."

"All right," he sighed, "I won't be mad at you."

"Would you mind, awfully, wearing a tie to church and to some of the more special events?"

It worked. He finally began to wear a tie, at least part of the time.

Everyone Loves A Bargain

Since it is very easy to see a mate's faults and super easy to excuse our own, you might have more success in getting your husband to see your point of view if you first let him know that you're going to do something about yourself.

You can say, "Darling, you know how you've been wanting me to learn how to balance the checkbook? Well, I've decided that, even though it's not what I enjoy doing, I'm going to do it, because I love you." The next week, after you've learned to balance the checkbook, you can come up with, "Hon, is there something else about me that you would like to see different?" He probably won't be able to think of a thing at the moment, so you can say, "I've really been trying to do things that will please you. Would you mind doing something that would please me, too?"

Be careful, though. This type of communication can get out of hand and deteriorate into manipulation. One couple shared that they use this method on each other in a rather unique way.

"I can get him to do anything by giving him sex," she told me. "I'll say, 'Honey, please go downtown with me.' He'll say, 'Okay, but you have to come in the bedroom first.' "

As I understand it, this is almost a daily thing with them. I asked, "Don't either of you resent being used this way?" They seemed to agree that it has worked fine for them. It wouldn't be my piece of pie.

If you bargain, keep your initial goal in mind. You are reaching for an ultimate good for him as well as yourself. If he refuses to cooperate, smile, kiss him, and say, "I'm going to go ahead with my part, even if you don't do yours, because I love you," and figure out some other way to reach him.

When You Consider His Ideas

If you plan to ask his advice about a matter, be prepared to take it. If you already have ideas of your own which you favor, prepare him for it by saying, "I think I know what I have to do that will be best for the situation, but I really would like your thoughts on the matter before I make my decision.''

When he does venture an opinion or idea, respond positively. If you think he's presented a bummer, you can be gracious enough to say "Hmmmm . . . thank you, Hon," letting him know you are at least considering it.

If his thoughts have possibilities, you can hug him and say, "You have the best ideas. I just might use them. If not this time, then another.''

Listen To His Heartbeat

One of the most intriguing personalities to appear on the world scene was Great Britain's Prime Minister, Margaret Thatcher. A woman who wants a high score in personal relationships would do well to note that Mrs. Thatcher was reported to possess a willingness to listen and discuss, rather than lecture. Initially, she captured the admiration of her nation by evidently attempting to hear the heartbeat of others and working to answer that heartbeat with workable solutions to overwhelming problems.

Clarice's marriage would have been doomed long ago if she hadn't learned to listen. It seems that her Darryl had been the son of transient workers, and as a little boy he enjoyed few of the necessities of life, let alone the luxuries. Not having the benefit of an education due to their nomadic existence, he grew up thinking he was dumb. The fact that he was able to catch up on his education later, finish college, and become a professional man still didn't take away that feeling of inadequacy.

When his son didn't show himself well in the academic field, Darryl became furious and verbally abusive and almost rejected the boy. Clarice understood what was behind it and coped as best as she could, building the boy up continually so the father's tearing down wouldn't destroy him. She tried to avoid open conflict with Darryl as much as possible, for it only made him act worse toward his son. Gradually he was able to accept his offspring, and although the child bears emotional scars of his own because of the former rejection, at least *now* he knows his father loves him.

You really owe it to your marriage to *listen* to what's inside that man of yours. Try to find out *why* he has certain feelings about any one given subject which might be causing conflicts between you, as we did with the man who refused to discuss family problems, mentioned in Chapter 5. Discovering dark influences in the past gives no man a right to use that as an excuse to continue making life miserable for others around him, but if you get to the root of the matter, you may be able to be more patient while he attempts to correct it.

Remembering the preparation steps we have already discussed, you can scrunch up close to your honey, and after sharing with him that you need him to help you in a particular matter, you might say, "It occurred to me that I may not be understanding your feelings about this—what's really keeping you from doing it. I think I've been so concerned about how it hurts *me* that I haven't been kind enough to think about how it hurts you. Maybe if I listened to how you feel about it, we could reach some sort of understanding — even a compromise."

If he says nothing, wait awhile, perhaps running your fingers gently through his hair or over his neck, and then say, "You haven't said anything yet."

If he still refuses to respond, kiss him and say, "Well, maybe you'll feel more like discussing it another day," and drop it for a few weeks. He might bring it up himself later on.

Rick wrote, "All I know is that for years I'll be against something, and then all of a sudden I'm in favor of it, just as my wife has been all the time." Smart wife. Happy husband.

Heart Check

If you're struggling with the idea of having to put out all that effort just for HIM, perk up! You'll benefit from it too. Let's find out if your reluctance might be stemming from a deeper problem. We aren't finished with Queen Esther, either.

7

WHAT'S MOVING
BEHIND YOUR TEETH?

One time I couldn't talk—at all. George and I had ministered the weekend before. Within two days we had appeared on national television, were interviewed on radio, were guest speakers for two groups, and had attempted to help a couple keep a marriage together that was screaming to fall apart, with that session lasting into the wee hours of one morning. With very little time to eat or sleep, plus two long flights from one coast to the other, we had a physical battle of health to fight when we got home. I lost part of it to laryngitis. It even hurt to whisper.

At dinner shortly after we returned, our daughter, at "that" age in her teen years, vigorously began to salt the asparagus blintz I had prepared. I silently but emphatically attempted to inform her that it was already salty. Her dad, realizing that I was trying to get a message across, said, "Honey, Mama says it's already salted."

She loudly returned, "I already tasted it! I ought to know if I should salt it again or not."

True to my mother instinct, I mouthed as definitely as I could, "Young lady that was rude."

My correction wasn't lost on her, for she returned, "Well, I have to defend myself when you yell at me."

"Yell!" George objected. "She can't even talk!"

She looked up from her plate to observe, "She doesn't have to say anything to yell."

It seemed like I was yelling because she didn't want to hear what I was saying. My inside voice was coming through loud and clear. Husbands are just teenagers grown bigger. When your husband thinks you talk too much, when you've barely gotten a sentence out, or when he believes you are clamorous and naggy when you aren't, it's sometimes because he doesn't want to hear about his shortcomings and responsibilities, especially from you. And sometimes his resentment may be because there is a lot more to your input than your words.

Negative Reactions

What comes out of the mouth verbally sometimes reflects deep conflict inside. If you have negative feelings, they will be reflected in attitudes that tell everyone around you a whole lot of things you don't think they know. And if you aren't very careful, they may turn into a seething caldron that will scald your life.

If, upon honestly listening to your voice, you realize that quite often it is cold, hard, bitter, sarcastic, flippant, blah, emotional, unemotional, angry, whiny, tearful, or quiet but lethal and sarcastic, it may indicate a hurt that is deeply entrenched in your conscious or subconscious mind. You may be wounded inside and it's blasting out through your larynx.

I asked one woman, "Do you hate your father?" Upon carefully considering the query, she answered, "Yes, I think I do." She went on to say that it had never occurred to her before, but the thought opened up new vistas of understanding as to some of the reasons why she resented her husband and was continually trying to badger him into changing his male characteristics that reminded her of not-so-dear-old Dad.

One woman was angry because she married a man who couldn't climb up to her level of expectation. Her father had been a successful professional man who had made life very comfortable for her when she was home, but her husband could do no better than manage a small tract home for her even after 15 years of marriage. Her disappointment not only kept their home in a negative uproar, but it turned her into such a compulsively meticulous housekeeper that you could eat off her floors and not get a speck of dust on your tomato.

Betty was another who was getting caught in a destructive web. She hadn't realized, until it was pointed out to her, that she was taking an opposite stand to everything her husband said. I ventured, "I think you're angry with your husband and this is how you show it." She replied, "Yes. I am angry with him. He has little respect for my ideas at all. What I say isn't important to him. I guess this is how I've been trying to get even with him."

But more probing revealed that her anger was not stemming so much from the fact that he had no respect for her ideas. He gave her plenty of opportunities to develop her abilities, and he encouraged her in them. What was burning her up was that he was paying too much attention to her teenage daughter from a former marriage, who was buttering up to Step-Pop. The result was almost total rejection by Mom. She was sure something immoral would happen in the future between the two of them, which she expressed to her husband more than once. She desperately needed him to shower romance on her, but what had already been a problem in that area was heightened because of her accusations and insinuations where the daughter was concerned, which he felt were totally unjustified.

We worked out some practical steps which she could take to kill the emotional monster that had gripped her thought life, and at the same time awaken her husband to his responsibility to put his wife first in his life without neglecting the daughter.

First, she was to quit mentioning the possibilities of sexual temptation to him where the girl was concerned. She had made her point too many times already, perhaps even making it more difficult for him to cope with his own feelings in that area.

Secondly, she would make an effort to spend time with the girl on a positive basis.

On family vacations (which she had grown to hate), she would make a point of spending some time each day just with her "adversary." Formerly, she had played only with the younger children and then suffered smoldering jealousy when the older one tagged along with Dad for companionship. In the future, she was to shout out an invitation to her daughter to race her to a tree, play hopscotch on the sand, or just walk off with her for some woman talk.

Thirdly, she would compliment the teenager, in private and in her husband's presence, mentioning the things she did well, instead of haranguing her about her inadequacies.

In this case, amazing results started taking place from the first hour of Betty's determination to turn the problem around! Not only did the daughter respond enthusiastically to the new show of love, but the father began to warm up to his wife romantically and their talk times became more productive when he saw her reaching out to the daughter. He began to make an effort to show his affection toward his wife in front of the daughter, thus putting her in her rightful place. The marriage relationship began to level out into normality and a deeper love began to flow between them.

Not Speaking To Him

The majority of the men we surveyed (See Chapter 5) came back with a thunderous NEVER in answer to our question, "Can your wife influence you to do something she wants by not speaking to you?" The horror of that was much worse in their minds than the idea of anger that burst all over them. I suppose it stems from the basic fear that we all have of being rejected. "Not speaking" is an insult to another person's very being, and any lady who indulges in it is not really acting like a lady at all.

One exception: you *should* refrain from speaking when you are about to lose control, and *should* leave the room until you are calm; the silence shouldn't go on for long, and you should let your husband know why you aren't talking. People who don't settle their differences before the day is out are going to have a marriage that is soon devoid of a warm, close, loving relationship.

Okay Once In Awhile?

We aren't talking about surface anger. A number of our "survey" men said they resist any show of anger, but over half of them felt that their wives needed to show surface anger sometimes in order to let them know they meant business. The men didn't mind that as long as it wasn't very often.

Fearful Lady

A woman with whom I dealt had come out of a first marriage where her husband had gambled them into poverty. She had such fears that she didn't trust her new mate in any way—finances, fidelity, or integrity. He wasn't without fault in these areas, but she yelled and screamed her way right into a second divorce, more fearful and insecure than ever.

There are lots of angry, fearful women in this world. Whether they are that way because of real or imagined injustices heaped upon them in their past or whether they are unduly influenced by the negative force perpetrated by our spiritual enemy that permeates every aspect of life, their ugliness spills out as if to consume everyone.

If you are one of them, no doubt you feel you have reason to be. But there is little excuse to continue it. It can make you ill. It can leave you wide open for disease. It's time to replace the rot inside with vibrant, new healing thoughts and action. To put it rather strongly, it's time to quit acting like a baby who doesn't get her way, and to start growing up. If you can't do it on your own, get help.

If your husband is the one with the problem of geyser action, try to determine why. It's important that you never give up on helping him do away with negatives in his life, any more than you should give up on conquering yours.

Heading It Off

If you don't have any skeletons in your closet to speak of, and your anger or fear is within the range of normal reaction, at least try to cut it down to a minimum. An active volcano may be beautiful to view, but a person feels relief when he moves out from under it. Before your mate decides to sail different seas, smooth the one he's on now by anticipating and conquering.

Nor is it fair to suggest that your husband is responsible for all your moods. Early in Pam and Ted's marriage she said to him, "Do you realize that every time I'm about to have a period, we get into a quarrel?"

He stopped, thought about it, and then burst out, "Of course! Why haven't I seen it? Of all the stupid jerks I am. I'll never let that happen again." And he didn't. He kept a record on his own calendar, so he could be extra patient during that time. Pam started marking the week before with big X's and the words WATCH OUT written across those days on her calendar so that she could be more pleasant when she felt like chewing everybody up.

Aside from anticipating the big monthly, there are other ways to avoid trouble:

. . . if you are cranky when you're tired, arrange a doze-off period during the day;

. . . keep your blood sugar up by eating something every two or three hours. (No stimulants, sugar, or white flour). They can make your blood sugar plummet later on and exhaust you. If you are overweight stick to non-fattening snacks);

. . . hum, sing, whistle, and look for the fun in the middle of rushing moments;

. . . anticipate your family's reaction by analyzing their habits and taking steps to avoid negative confrontations as much as possible;

. . . if you feel emotions rising, force your reluctant self to get involved in a different activity: walk around the house a few times, stopping to enjoy bits of nature; go into the bathroom, lock the door, and read a magazine article, or write a letter.

Doomsday Dilly

It's pretty hard to influence a husband to do something happy for you if you are never sunshine. Women who are constantly negative remind their husbands of the proverbial Chinese water torture—drip, drip, drippety drip.

Some people are negative by nature, it seems. Francie moaned to her husband and everyone else about the fact that her job was boring. She wasn't given enough to do. It was the same old thing, over and over. She didn't know how long she could stand it.

"I wish I didn't have to stand around so much," she'd say.

When I saw her again recently I smiled broadly: "Looks like you got your wish, Francie. I've never seen this office so busy."

Her chin dropped and she looked sadder than ever as she confided, "Yes. Too busy, if you ask me. I don't have time to do anything but work."

Terrance tried. He really did. He would cheerfully counteract his wife's gloominess by pointing out the happy side of any given situation. He'd laugh when he was tempted to cry. He was happiness and sunshine itself, despite the boulder of a wife that was tied around his neck. And when she died, he was genuinely sorrowful, for he had such a good attitude that he really did love her. But it wasn't long until he began to enjoy the new, light-filled existence that was now his, and before too long he found a wife who filled his life with the happiness he had deserved long before.

If you are a rainy cloud, it's time to turn off the spigot. You might consider setting up a daily practice schedule like a singer does for vocalizing. During that period, consciously turn every negative thought into a positive one. Or play a game all day as you hurry along. Find something good in everything that happens. If you learn to dwell on your blessings with a thankful heart, you'll have very little time to hang your hat on that which weighs you down and everyone else around you.

Learn to look upon negative reactions as poison to your mind, your body, and your relationships, so you can avoid them like you avoid eating household cleaner. If you do blow up, apologize—out loud—in a grownup, ladylike way.

Tears

How about other typical female reactions to a disappointing male? My survey showed that more men are moved by tears than by anger, especially if they come from an honest "broken heart."

As we look at Queen Esther again, we see that she finally showed her femaleness by shedding tears to get what she wanted. Although King Ahasuerus had ordered Haman hung on the gallows, although he had given all of Haman's possessions to Esther to do with as she saw fit, and although he had handed over Haman's ring to Mordecai (making that nice fellow second only to the king over all the kingdom), the Jews were still doomed, simply because any command signed by the king could not be reversed, not even by him. That was the law.

So Esther still had some communicating to do, but this time she took a shortcut. She had been so successful up to that point and her confidence was so greatly increased, that she didn't wait on ceremony or consider her fate as carefully as before. Instead, she walked straight into the throne room, fell down at the king's feet, and shed some royal tears. Perhaps the monarch, in the tender moments that undoubtedly followed the demise of Haman and the establishing of Mordecai, had given her blanket permission to come to him anytime if she had a serious problem.

At any rate, with wet drops finding their way down her lovely cheeks, she besought him to reverse what Haman had done. He raised his golden scepter, whereupon Esther stood up, and remembering that blubbering shouldn't be continued, gained control of herself and, with nary an invitation to the king for dinner, she started over, speaking respectfully and with complimentary words. Having shown the king that she recognized who he was, she continued, stating her cause outright.

Although the king was sympathetic, he couldn't change the law. Somehow he had to figure some way around what he had ordered. But what?

So what happened? Were the Jews slaughtered, as they later were in Hitler's regime? Was Esther spared? I'm not going to tell you. If you want to know how Ahasuerus handled that very difficult situation, take a few minutes to read it in the Book of Esther in the Old Testament of your Bible. The king's solution is recorded in chapter 8 of Esther. I wouldn't be surprised if you read right to the end of that little bit of history, and then flip back to the beginning to take in details of what I've related to you. It's a fascinating account of an ancient kingdom.

Humor And Teasing

Unlike Ahasuerus, however, some men have no sympathy with tears whatsover. If your fella is like that, try the funny approach. Walt shared, ''My wife can get me to do almost anything by asking with a smile in her voice and a twinkle in her eye. Sometimes she even teases me into it.'' Of course a queenly person wouldn't put barbs in her teasing. That would be nothing more than veiled hostility.

What Others Hear

Maybe your voice isn't reflecting any deep, nasty feelings at all, but your honey may have tuned you out simply because he's had it with its irritating sound! Like a woman who wears dirty clothes and has unkempt hair is one who pays no attention to the sounds she makes. Take stock. Although you need to be *you* and not try to be something you are not, there's no law against a little refinement. Ask yourself some questions:

Do I Talk Too Loudly Most of the Time?

A woman can very quickly lose two of her greatest assets, her charm and femininity, if she bellows like a calliope. Except for occasional deviations, a loud-voiced doll, or one who explodes noisily, can be an embarrassment to her husband and an audible threat to his need to be a dominant, masculine male. You can teach yourself to tone down if you are inclined toward this type of melody-making. Learning to speak pleasingly is one of the first things they would drum into you if you attended a high-priced finishing school. Learn it yourself. You can practice while you are alone, and then carry it over into response to your family.

Do I Resemble a Mouse?

Dick was representative of a number of husbands when he complained to me, ''I wish my wife would speak up. I feel our marriage is getting humdrum because she's so afraid to share her ideas.''

Like the doormat wife, you can lose your husband's respect if you speak fearfully or so meekly that you have no assertiveness or personality in your voice.

If your soft voice brims with strength, however, and your husband has tuned out conversationally, it may be because he simply doesn't hear you half the time. Perhaps it's too much of a strain to listen. You might consider taking lessons from someone who has worked with the speaking voice, so that you can learn to project.

Does My Voice Have an Edge to It?

Some people have sensitive hearing and find it difficult to tolerate certain sounds or loud noises. I'm one of them. I like big chunks of quiet and enjoy it at home when I'm alone. I play no radio, watch no TV, and talk on the telephone only when necessary.

My mother was a schoolteacher before I made my acquaintance with her at my birth, and a substitute teacher after I arrived on the scene. I often sat under her tutelage in the absence of a regular instructor. She kept marvelous control of any age group in the classroom. Although her voice wasn't loud, she spoke in a ringing, authoritative way that left no doubt in anyone's mind who was in charge. In the classroom I could handle it, but at home there were times when her voice set my ears buzzing. If she was angry with me, the edge seemed even sharper. If I would say, "Mama, you hurt my ears!" her big, beautiful blue eyes would flash and I would *really* get a tongue-lashing. That was because she felt I was just trying to hush her up, and disrespectful children weren't tolerated in our home very well at all!

Perhaps your voice grates on your husband's ears. Learn to speak with a relaxed jaw, an open throat, and open nasal passages, mentally placing the sound behind the bridge of the nose. A rounder, fuller tone will result.

You might check the other sound levels in your home, too. My husband enjoys music going all the time. He doesn't mind the blaring of our children's stereo, either. But because he is sensitive to my needs, he plays the radio at a low volume or not at all, and doesn't interfere when I turn their stereos down. You might do the same for your love.

But that isn't all. Here's another query which should come from you to you:

Am I a Nonstop Talker?

The nonstopper can drive a good man to stony silence or a cheerful escape. He can nod and say "Uh huh" and "Hmmm" without breaking a single link in his chain of thought, which has nothing to do with the barrage of words pouring out of his companion. You really *don't* have to say everything that's on your mind, you know. You can leave out details. It's also socially acceptable and quite healthy to take a few breaths and pause a bit before going on. Just plain silence between a husband and wife can be pregnant with good, meaningful communication.

One high-speed communicator I know was married to a man who is mentally brilliant but slow and awkward in expressing himself verbally. While he was forming an answer to one of her questions, she would go on to several other subjects. There were other reasons besides her voice, but he divorced her this year.

Numerous wives have told me that when they quit talking so much, their husbands who were once poor communicators began to open up.

Are My Subjects Interesting?

Do I drivel on about trivia? Although some simple chatter is a relaxer for men occasionally, if you talk on the level of an elementary schoolchild, your husband may forget how to treat you like a woman.

It's well to remember, too, that as a rule husbands get upsy in the stomach when they hear about things like how many times Buster Baby messed his pants (or worse) today. And even though you think you need his sympathy, the fact that you have terrible cramps from your period or indigestion is bound to dampen his day and his ardor.

Heart Check

Perhaps you're saying, "But I have to be ME!" Sometimes what I think is "ME" is just a product of habits and environmental teachings over the years. Some personality traits we acquire and nurse are simply out of place. Do a makeup job on your heart so that your approaches to your husband will be of prime quality. Then if communication doesn't get the job done, move on to the next step—coming up!

8

STEP FOUR— SPELL IT OUT WITH ACTION

◆━━━━━━━━━━━━━━━━━━━━━━

There is many a time when verbalizing a gripe has no more effect on a husband than a weed in the neighborhood's yard. You can talk until you are blue, pink, and red in the face but he blithely goes on doing as he did before you started, even though he may cheerfully agree that he ought to make some changes.

In such a case, it's time to spell out your need with action that will convince him that you aren't playing games. Because they are common gripes, we're going to spend the next few chapters looking at what you can *do* to help the man around your house see the light of day regarding:

> Sweet thoughtfulness
> Sex
> Physical abuse and adultery
> Money
> Doing his share in and out
> of the house

Sweet Thoughtfulness

A lady with many years of frustration behind her wrote, "I am one of thousands of wives who are in some kind of limbo. I have all the responsibilities and difficulties of marriage without the joys and privileges which should accompany them. I'm sure my husband loves me, but you'd never know it by any action or word of *his*."

In direct contrast is this note I received from Charlotte:

> My husband, for 46 years, was the most gentlemanly, loving, complimentary, romancing man I ever knew. A diamond was presented for each child (there were seven). Gifts and flowers were regular offerings on all occasions. He never forgot birthdays and anniversaries. He was always kind, always considerate, always handled me with care, sexually, as though I was a delicate flower that breath would wisp away. When he came in from work, his coat went on a hall hanger. He rolled up his sleeves and helped me in whatever my unfinished task might be.

Many women would be envious of that woman's blessings. But don't despair if the one with whom you live doesn't measure anywhere near to her standard. Do something about it.

One friend wrote that she longed to have her husband be more romantic, but each time she tried to tell him, it was so important to her that she would break down and cry. That confused the issue even more. He just didn't understand what she was talking about.

Although there are a few stalwart men who won't change anything they are doing for anybody, we've been amazed at how many are willing to become more like the knight in shining armor that their brides envisioned them to be if someone will just show them how to go about it, and what to do. Unfortunately, men don't seem to pick it up very readily from their wives.

Consider Then:

Getting him out to a marriage seminar that has a reputation for stressing women's needs as much as men's. You can ascertain that by asking about content material from others who have attended before;

Asking your pastor to preach a series of sermons on women's needs that husbands should supply. He has access to much research material on the subject. If not, give him some;

Asking your Sunday school or Bible class teacher to have a few lessons on the husband's responsibilities to the wife;

Supplying your husband with articles you've found on the subject. Hand them to him with the assurance that you are reading material on how to be a better wife;

Handing him books to read that cover the subject. There are several good ones on the market now, and since my purpose is to help you make your marriage better, I won't hesitate to recommend mine.

She Giggled In Bed

One woman wrote, "My husband and I always sit up in bed at night for a little while reading before we go to sleep. I knew he wouldn't read your book *Forever My Love* (What Every Man Should Know About His Wife) if I asked him to, so I started reading it instead. I didn't say anything. I just laughed, giggled, gasped, and exclaimed until finally he looked at me, grinning wonderingly, and asked, 'What's so funny?' I replied, 'Listen to this,' and I read a portion to him. He chuckled, too. After awhile he looked at me again as I reacted out loud, so I read some more to him. Night after night I did this. It's worked. He's so much more understanding and attentive now."

Another woman called me, saying that she had read an interview in her city newspaper about me. "I just wanted you to know that I ran down, got your book, and asked my husband to read it. He did an about-face. We stopped our divorce, handed the book to our psychiatrist, and fired him. I didn't know marriage could be so wonderful."

One happy fellow ran clear down the aisle of the church, threw his arms around me, whirled me around, and laughed, "Thank you, thank you, for making our marriage a heaven on earth!" I had never met the man before, and I was curious to know what had happened. He said, "My wife brought your book home, see, and the first I remember seeing it was on my bedstand. I ignored it. The next thing I knew it was staring me in the face beside my coffee cup. I shoved it aside. It showed up by my shaving gear, and in my briefcase. I finally read it to get her off my back. I wish I'd started on this stuff 15 years ago! You'll never know what a difference it has made in our marriage."

A gentleman who was *very* tall walked up to me one day, looked down on the top of my head, and said, "I read your book, and I . . . just . . . (he was searching for a word that would describe how disdainful he felt) . . . *tossed* it out!" A week later he reappeared. Over he marched. I peered up, up, up as he said, "I read your book again. It's got a few good things in it." Third week—same fellow. "That book of yours. I've read it again. You know, I found some things I could agree with you about." Fourth week: "I've decided you've got some pretty good things in that book . . . uh, I read it again." The fifth week, he romped up to me, buoyantly happy. "Terrific book! I've started doing some of the things you suggest, and has my wife ever changed!"

Whether it's a book you influence him to read, or a place you and he go so he can hear what you long to have him hear, always remember that the best way to get a mule to dig in his hooves and not move is to get him thinking that you're trying to force him to do something.

Planting The Seed

Turning a stubborn mule into one willing to cooperate can be accomplished by planting seeds. Internationally known psychologist Dr. Clyde Narramore (See Chapter 1) suggests this as well.

Let's say your church or some other organization is sponsoring a series of lectures on marriage. Your man may think of 94 reasons why he couldn't possibly go, and if you keep pushing it, he may just say, "I am *not* going!" So forget it. He isn't going. If you bully him into it, he won't be receptive anyway.

Be more clever than that. If he's in church, he'll probably hear the announcement. If not, you can take a brochure home and leave it on the kitchen table. If he doesn't notice it, pick it up in his presence, read it silently, and say,

"Hmmm. Well, what do you know?" As soon as he turns his attention to your hmm's, say, "They're having a series of meetings on marriage at our church—in June." Then change the subject.

Maybe two weeks after that, be looking at it again and comment, "You know, this seminar might be worth attending. I've heard it's very good."

A few days later feed a little more information into his computer, like, "Bill and Clara went once. They said it was the smartest thing they ever did. And they have a good marriage, too. It wouldn't hurt me to learn how to be a better wife. They prefer husbands and wives attending together, though. It would be good for both of us." Pause. Let it sink in. "It doesn't cost an awful lot considering how much it is to go out to dinner. We'd get our money's worth, that's for sure."

The next week try, "Honey, I would just love it if we could go to that seminar together. I couldn't bear to go without you. I'd be terribly lonely without you." If he still isn't receptive, you can sacrifice something. Perhaps, "I'd be willing to not go out to dinner for a month, if we could go. How about it? Besides, you have such good insights and sometimes catch important truths that escape me." And that's true, isn't it?

You might even have the money all saved for it, so he won't use that as an excuse. The important part of preparing him for going is not to give him the idea that you want him to go because *he* needs it, but rather that you *both* need it.

Planting seed can be effective in many areas of your relationship.

If You Want To Get Away

Mini-vacations are a wonderful means of pumping some sweet thoughtfulness back into your lives. If you've forgotten, in your busyness, how to be super-feminine, how to lean on your man's masculine strength, or how to be charming, getting by yourselves away from distractions can do wonders to bring it all back to you. And that tends to usher the chivalry back into the thinking of your darling.

You may recall my mentioning that some men told me they wished their wives would give them more attention (Chapter 6). Children, homekeeping, and activities seem to get it all. If you capitalize on that need he feels he has, he will probably agree that it would be great to get away. His desires will start flowing if you suggest a half-dozen places you could go, backing yourself up with travel folders. If romantic spots are within driving distance, ask the resort or hotel to send a brochure on their facilities. Know the costs and be ready to show him how affordable it is (you will have chosen within your budget) and what fun it will be.

You might start the conversation like this: "You know, I love our children, and I enjoy our friends. We have a nice home, too. But I feel a real need to get you all to myself for awhile, so I can just love you to pieces and you can love me to pieces. I want to shower attention on you, which I can't do now because I'm pulled so many different ways. And I'd love it if no one else was around to get *your* attention. I'd like to do things with you like when we were on our first honeymoon. I *miss* you. Do you think we could get away for a few days alone?''

That sort of getting away can get to be a very happy habit. Dolores' husband took her on 35 wonderful honeymoons. He started saving quarters their first year of marriage and used them to pay for each trip. Then when quarters couldn't keep up with inflation, and could no longer pay the expenses, he would take them along, give her half, keep half himself, and on their trip they would each spend them as they wished.

When They Put It Off

Some men procrastinate so much that if you wait for them to decide to go somewhere, you'll be waiting until the day of your funeral. Phyllis solved that. Dan said that they had long discussed the idea of going to Canada to visit some relatives there, but he couldn't ever quite get around to making it definite. Finally, after some years, she simply wrote to the relatives, set some dates, worked out the travel and finance arrangements, and then wisely waited until just the right moment to tell Dan about it. Since it was all done, he had no reason to put it off any longer. They went, and had a wonderful time.

Many men are far more receptive when the groundwork is laid so they don't have to think about it too much. Mary is all ready for her husband when she wants to go out. She will ask, ''Wouldn't it be fun to go to a play soon? Look, there are three good ones playing right now.''

She has already taken the effort to find out what they are about, what the reviews have said, and when tickets are available, so if he asks any questions, the answers are at her fingertips. Sometimes she'll read the review out loud to him and ask, "Does it sound like something you would enjoy?"

When He Takes You For Granted

Kathy was getting upset because she felt her husband was assuming too much. He would say, "Let's go to a ball game this weekend." If she agreed, he'd leave her with a parting shot—"Get the tickets, Hon." Now that wouldn't bother some women. They'd just be glad he wanted to go and called them "Hon." But it bothered her because, as she said, "He wouldn't have thought of doing that when we were going together." But his ears were closed to her pleas. One time, when they decided they'd like to go to the Ice Follies, he did the same as before, and on the evening they were to go, he came shooting home from work, ready to take off.

"Ready, Babe?" he called, "Got the tickets?"

"No, I don't," she answered seriously.

"You don't? What happened?"

"I just didn't get them, that's all. I need you to think of me as special enough and someone you care enough about to make arrangements for our dates, just like you used to."

They didn't get to go to the Ice Follies, but her firm reminder struck home. From then on he made arrangements, secured the tickets, and properly escorted her to wherever they were going.

If that frightens you, perhaps this approach by a widow who had been married for many years to a very successful author and who was a professional woman herself, won't:

I always approached my husband with the idea that WE had a problem, not just me. It was never "I need, and therefore you must" but "We need, so let's see if we can work out the solution to this problem of ours."

At one time in our relationship I would prepare his breakfast, and then, before I could sit down to enjoy it with him, he had eaten and left the room, with not a word. Finally I said to him, "We have a difficulty. Let's see if we can work it out." As soon as I had his ear, I said, "We have to do things together if we are to remain close to each other. When you leave the table before I can join you, we aren't together." He responded.

This same delightful lady shared that since her husband was an indecisive man, planning a time out together could be torturous, so, "*We* worked out a solution. *We* decided that since *we* felt *we* should get out together at least once a week, *we* would set it up on a basis of 'You decide this week. I decide next week.' He loved the seashore and I loved the mountains, so we compromised even further. On even days we would go to the mountains, on odd days the seashore." All he had to decide was which seashore spot he'd prefer enjoying.

If He Leaves You Sitting

Golf widow? The dear who's left behind while he's hunting? Gather your knitting needles, your scrapbook materials, the reading you need to catch up on, and insist on going with him sometimes, if you can't get him to compromise with "my-choice-now-your-choice." Even better, purchase some golf clubs and a gun. Watch his admiration rise to new heights as you learn, from a proper teacher, how to be a real Annie Oakley on the course or in the woods.

If you are a definite second choice to the boys, perhaps he simply needs to get away from you occasionally. Togetherness is wonderful, but too much sugar in a cake can make some people sick to the stomach. Take advantage of the freedom! Do something with some of the lonely single women that pine away in their apartments (naturally you will not include other men in your plans); pursue a mini-career with college classes or home study; go wild on your hobby.

I Want Him To Say Sweet Things

Nicole's husband wasn't about to get his feet wet with romantic goo. He's a fellow who never saw love between his parents because they divorced when he was young. He finds it difficult to even say "I love you." We watched one evening, amused, when it was time for them to go home from a party.

He said, "Honey, let's go."

She returned, "Okay, Dear." But she sat still and kept on talking.

After awhile he said, "Honey, we've got to go."

All right, Sweetheart.'' She kept on talking.

This went on for some time. Finally, exasperated, he said, ''Honey, didn't you hear me?''

She turned to him, sparkling with affection, and said, ''Of course I heard you. It's just that I love to hear you call me 'Honey,' and the longer I sit here the more times I get to hear it.''

She'll say, ''Why do you love me? Give me three reasons.'' Even though she doesn't get to hear the three little words themselves, this approach does get him to thinking, and some very nice ''reasons'' come out of his mouth.

Teach By Example

Some husbands learn by osmosis. If you call *him* sweet names, he may start saying them to you. It can get a little out of hand, of course. One family I know is so open with loving each other that anyone or anything that comes in sight, including the cat, the dog, and the bird, are dubbed ''Honey,'' ''Sweetheart,'' ''Lover,'' and anything else that pops into their minds. But don't knock it. It's a lot better than a growl, or ignoring someone.

Compliments

If you look your best (usually) and he remains mute, try meeting him at the door some evening with your hair tousled, an unbecoming outfit, no perfume, no makeup, the house in shambles, and the kids dirty.

If he says anything, you can come back with, ''Oh, you noticed. Well, tomorrow I'll have it different, and if you like, I'll keep it that way.'' If he compliments you the next day on the change, thank him and let him know in some special way that you appreciate it. Serve him a dessert he likes, give him an evening of lovemaking, etc. If he says nothing, you can ask, "Which way did you like me and your home—today's way or yesterday's?"

"Today's," he's bound to answer.

"I'm sure you do. It takes a lot of effort to look nice for you, to make sure the house is sparkling and the kids are clean. But you rarely show any appreciation. I don't treat you like that, and I don't want to be treated like that either." If you get no response even after several tries, drop the idea before you get upset, and try something else.

Gifts

Women love gifts—little, big, small. It doesn't matter. It's the idea that to them gifts mean "You love me." But face it —although some smart fellows regularly come into home plate in this way, others are so far out in left field that the ball gets lost altogether.

Tina finally had to buy herself gifts on special days, as a start-him. Very *expensive* gifts. When he nearly fainted as he peeked at the price tags, she said, "I only get them so I can pretend they're from the man I love. That's you. If you want to get me gifts, you won't have to pay as much. It would assure me that you really love me." Although her stubborn suitor still forgets upon occasion or figures it's too much trouble, he has improved and she does get gifts.

Set The Kids To Work

I was in a large department store one day

before Christmas and heard a mother call quietly to her son, who looked to be about nine years old.

"Troy," she whispered, "look at those beautiful boxes of soaps and bubble bath. You can tell Daddy I'd love one of those for Christmas." He nodded knowingly and said, "I gotcha, Mom." Knowing little boys, he probably went home and counted his own pennies as well to see if he could possibly afford such a lovely gift himself for the love of his life, his mother, or else he talked Daddy into sharing with him on it.

Insecure?

At least two women who answered my surveys found out that the reason why their husbands didn't buy them anything was that they felt their wives wouldn't like what they picked out. Perhaps that was the reaction they got from their mothers when they were growing up, when they gave them a gift. I've known wives, too, who have trotted right down to the store with the gifts their husbands picked out and got something they'd like better. I think maybe some people have forgotten the meaning of the word "gift."

Lisa's husband felt insecure about buying anything for her. So they agreed that when gift time came around they would go together. If she saw something she liked, he would get it for her. Other families solve the problem with list-making. Sometimes that's essential in this day of opulence and abundance.

Take Off On Your Own

The methods used by the women to encourage husbands to practice sweet thoughtfulness, which you just read about, are intended to be only a springboard for you to go sailing into the air in a beautiful swan dive with techniques of your own.

And while you are waiting for him to become inspired, generate more romance yourself. Just because he doesn't is no sign you shouldn't. You'll enjoy it, he probably will too, and it will instill some appreciation for the finer things of life in your children.

Heart Check

If his response was zero to romance, you'll only make matters worse by responding with ungracious emotions. Down with them! Up and onward with a song on your lips and hope in your heart.

9

HELP HIM BECOME AN IRRESISTIBLE LOVER

◆————————————————————

Probably one of the most universal beliefs is that women must *never* withhold sex from their husbands, except in the most extreme circumstances, like being in the hospital or dying. Any woman who would think of such a ghastly possibility, it is inferred, deserves all the punishment she can get, even that of her husband having an affair or divorcing her. I suppose we've heard it so much because most of the writers and preachers on the subject have been men.

Sheila said to me, "There comes a time when that's all the defense you have left." Many women feel this way, but they receive little sympathy.

Submission—To What?

The Bible gets pounded a lot on the submission passages to prove that withholding sex is a crime. We read in Ephesians 5:22, "Wives, submit yourselves unto your own husbands. . . ." Biblically oriented women aren't against that. What bothers many women who have talked with me is that the other Scriptures which would balance this out are ignored or minimized. Look at the verse just preceding, for instance. It says, "Submit to one another . . ."! Does that include everyone *but* husbands and wives? Obviously not. If a husband is to submit himself to his wife as well as her submitting to him, we have to ask, "In what way?" Naturally, there can't be two people filling the headship position, which has been given to the husband by God. That merely causes confusion for everybody in the home.

The search for the answer takes us right to another passage: "The husband must always give his wife what is due her" (1 Corinthians 7:3). The following verse says, "Do not deprive each other except by mutual consent" (NIV). What, then, is due a wife and how could a man deprive her? I have heard men expound excitedly to discouraged women, "That means that I'm not to deny you sex! At any time!" Wow, wow! He's got another excuse for sex on demand, and she's got another reason for disliking it.

He hasn't understood because he's lifting verses out of context. In the King James Version of the Bible, 1 Corinthians 7:3 is alternately rendered, ". . . her due benevolence," which fits in beautifully with 1 Peter 3:7, where it says the husband is to understand and honor his wife. Her emotional and physical needs are not in the same vein as his (see Chapter 2 of this book). He is to give her what is due her! Love! With or without sex. Attention! Sweet thoughtfulness! She is an individual, and though he has power over her body by rights given him by God, so has she power over his body by rights given her by God, so that she can, scripturally, say no sometimes if it is in the best interests of the marriage.

A man gives love to a woman, to a great extent, so she will satisfy him sexually. A woman gives sex to a man so he will satisfy her need for love. God intended that couples provide for each other. The wife reaches out for her need to be satisfied emotionally so she can *enjoy* the physical relationship as well as *enjoy* fulfilling the need of her husband. Happy is the man who gets his priorities straight on that one!

Think It Through

There's nothing that kills romance and love in a relationship faster than a woman getting to the point where she feels used. A man who insists on sex purely for the sake of relieving himself, with no regard to his wife's feelings, so that her ardor begins to cool, is asking for a turned-off or even frigid wife. A woman who doesn't educate her husband regarding the necessity of keeping romance alive is no less guilty.

But if she is wise, she will begin her education program with caution and in a queenly fashion, as described in the preceding chapters. If she lashes out at him in anger, locks the bedroom door, flounces into another room, denounces his ability to make love, or in other ways attacks his person, if she slams a book down in front of him that explains her position and demands indignantly that he read it, nothing but T-R-O-U-B-L-E will result.

You Have A Brain For A Reason

So, use it. The underlying *reason* for getting your husband to change his sexual approach must always be kept in mind: you are helping him meet your needs so that he will be the kind of husband God intended him to be, which in turn makes it easier for you to meet his needs, which in turn will give you a happier, stronger marriage. Therefore, the motivating emotions must be love and kindness, mixed with patience and accentuated by firmness. You must always keep in mind that sexual rejection by a wife can be extremely devastating to a man.

Since his image of macho male may have to be adjusted, you will have to start with the ABC's. Gradually, over a *long* period, you will want to get these points across to him:

1) I love you and want to keep loving you. You love me and I want you to keep loving me.

2) I love your body and I want to keep loving what you do to me with it. I can't risk spoiling that by letting you get in the habit of ignoring my needs.

3) In order for me to keep responding to you sexually, I must feel as if I am important to you as a person, not just a receptable.

4) I feel I am important to you when you treat me with sweet thoughtfulness throughout each day even when we don't make love.

5) My needs are to keep romance alive, which cannot be when my body is to be presented upon demand to you, whether I feel like it or not.

6) To keep romance alive, every lovemaking session should be given our best in the effort to please each other, not just one of us. We should make love, not just have sex. Otherwise, we will tire of each other,

and you will be tempted to seek out other women.

7) It's because I want each time to be exciting that I am not going to be available every moment you want my body.

Your husband will have to be gently reminded of the preceding many times. If you are consistent, however, he will begin to see what you mean, and will learn to love it if you make certain that your lovemaking is a thriller every time for him and for you. If he says something like, "It gets better every time," you can point out to him that it is because now you enjoy it, whereas before it was a duty.

Refusing Kindly

On any given occasion, you can say, "I'm sorry, Sweetheart, but I just don't feel like making love. I haven't felt like anybody special to you all day, or yesterday either. It would be really nice, though if we could make a date for tomorrow or the next night, so we can treat each other just like we used to before we were married. Then we'll both enjoy it more."

Or, if lack of romance isn't what's turning you off, state kindly and gently what it is. You can precede it with, "Darling, I know I'm a weakling sometimes, and a pain to you, but I can't make love tonight, because I've got a pain, too. I'm hurting inside, and it just takes away all my desire."

He'll undoubtedly respond with something like, "Hurting inside?"

Then tell him what's bothering you. For example:

Stinky Feet

Della wrote, "I just can't bear to have him make love to me anymore, because he has athlete's foot and refuses to wash his feet. The smell when he takes off his socks is unbearable. He won't get help for this repulsive disease either."

It's pretty hard to be sexually charming and eager about your husband's body when he has stinky feet. Among other things, we suggested that she buy her husband some foot powder and sprinkle it into his socks, so that when he puts them on, it will not only dispel the smell, but will keep his feet drier and possibly solve the athlete's foot problem. It has worked for many men who picked up the disease in the war. It feels good on the feet too.

Another suggestion was that she do what one very lovely wife did with her husband in a similar situation. (You read about Betty on the first page of this book). One evening, when Frank was changing, she came to him with a basin of warm, perfumed water and a towel. She said, "I pray that this will minister to you." She then proceeded to wash his feet lovingly.

It's a very humbling experience to have someone wash your feet. Her husband enjoyed it very much, although he was chagrined that she had to go to such extremes to convince him that this was important to her. Now they wash each other's feet from time to time, just as a symbol of love.

When He's Not Interested

If there are times when *you* would like to

make love and he can't or is disinclined, tuck that information away in your mind. Then, on one of the nights when you refuse him, and he acts unhappy about it, you can tease gently, "You should complain. I was rejected last time!" That will make him feel better as he realizes that giving as well as taking is normal.

Don't Get Carried Away

There's a limit to denying a man. A woman who leaves her bed is inviting another to step into it. You don't put him off for long, nor do you refuse to give him any idea of when you will want to make love. Most men need relief physically from time to time. If too often they are denied sexual relations, they might be tempted to consider other women or masturbation.

One mistaken matron, who was sharing her problems with me, thought she would prefer the latter and asked, "Why can't he masturbate instead of bothering me all the time? I despise it." She hadn't attempted to educate her husband regarding her needs or tried to enjoy their sexual times together, but later, she felt very sorry for herself and complained bitterly when he left her.

Understanding Him

God made man a sexual being. Although many men learn to control the drive by filling their minds with other pursuits, others see no need. A truck driver who delivered some books to our house one day expressed it very well, by sharing, "When I see a dame, right away I ask myself, 'I wonder what she'd be like in bed?' I can't see why my wife couldn't understand that. In fact it made her so mad, she left me. Why?" I suspect there may have been more to the story than he told me, but his "Why?" was sincere.

When you have denied your husband your body in the manner suggested, you might *initiate* the next lovemaking session yourself. A number of men wrote me that they wished their wives would be sexually aggressive sometimes. It makes them feel desired and loved, and it relieves their anxiety about how their wives view them.

How Often Is Often Enough?

After studying several surveys which handled the question of sex frequency in the bonds of marriage, including *Redbook Magazine's Sexual Pleasure: The Surprising Preferences of 100,000 Women,* the La Hayes' *Family Life Seminars Sexual Involvement Survey, Family Circle Magazine's The Sexual Stages of Marriage* and my own Margie Ministries' *Men's Survey and Women's Survey,* I can only come to the conclusion that happily married couples have sex within a range of not-at-all to 12 or more times a month. Those within this group who insist on extremes at either end of the sex-frequency scale are in a definite minority.

All the surveys point to the fact that every happily married couple manages to work out a frequency solution that is pleasing to both partners. The satisfaction that comes from their sexual relationship is not dependent on trying to fit into statistics. As in all aspects of life, each set of individuals is unique and should not pattern its responses to each other after someone else's lifestyle (beyond using others as a general guide).

Two noteworthy aspects: the surveys conducted by *Redbook,* the La Hayes, and myself showed very clearly that religious women enjoy sex more than those who are not religious. The La Hayes go even further, noting that those couples who pray regularly together have a definite edge in sexual enjoyment over those who seldom or never pray. This brings us right back to the One who started it all in the first place, doesn't it? It behooves us to consider *all* Scripture regarding the marriage relationship, of which sex is a part, and to follow the guidelines we find there.

Secondly, poor verbal communication lessens sexual enjoyment and understanding between partners. A lady who "just can't talk" with her husband about her sexual needs, expecting him to fly blind instead of guiding him, will suffer the consequences.

Same Old Time, Same Old Place

Just as it's doltish to have sex at the same time and on the same day repeatedly, so is it most unimaginative to confine yourself to the same spot. The old great-grandmotherish saying that variety is the spice of life is still true.

Throw away your embarrassment at setting up a love nest somewhere else right in your own home, when the children aren't around, and surprise the shoes off your husband by entering it as a sexy *femme fatale*. He'll *love* you for your desire to make your times with him special, and when he expresses his appreciation, even if it's only with shining eyes, you can let him know that this is a result of being so happy that he is trying to please you in other areas of your married life—one of those things on your list, maybe.

Colored Sheets

A friend of mine observed that men are competitive, so she capitalized on that in getting her husband, Bob, to be more creative in their lovemaking. It was very important to her for more than the fact that she just enjoyed it. She had a guilty conscience. During their first year of marriage, she had nearly killed his attempts at romance. He would kiss her on the back of the neck and she'd say, "Don't get any ideas. I'm tired." If he brought a gift, she'd comment, "It would have been so much prettier in blue. Didn't they have blue?" So he gave up.

Gradually, she won back his enthusiasm by rather extreme methods. One evening, she tacked colored sheets up to the ceiling of their bedroom, so the bed was a cozy hideaway. Flames danced from candles on the bureau. Flowers perfumed the air. She wrapped herself in one of the sheets. He was so excited about it that he tried some ideas of his own. One time, for example, when she flew to another city to meet him, she was greeted in the motel room with bumper stickers stuck everywhere—the ceiling, the walls, in the bathtub. They all read THINK BOB! The fact that he had gone to all that trouble delighted her no end, and she let him know it.

Little Helps

You could use these ideas that other women have tried with success:

Lay a comforter on the floor, encircling it with fresh flowers;

Set up a "Roman" atmosphere. Have bowls of small fresh fruit around, like grapes, to drop into your lover's mouth, and two wreaths of fresh flowers to slip on your heads;

Set an Oriental dinner on the coffee table, replete with pillows on the floor to sit on. After you eat, turn the lights off and light the candles and a perfume lamp. Then slip off an outer garment to reveal a very provocative one underneath.

With a little imagination and a scrutinizing look through your house you won't need anyone else to tell you how to make a man glad he's home.

Hints for exciting lovemaking are in both of our books, *Forever My Love* and *How to Enrich Your Marriage.* I won't repeat them here, but since their publication a few concerns have been voiced to us in person and by letter that were not dealt with in the books, so I include them now.

Enjoy It—Out Loud

Several men who wrote told us that they like their wives to relay their enjoyment to them audibly. Your husband might become much more enthusiastic about pleasing you if you let him know that he's doing all right as a lover by contented sighs, ''Mmmm's,'' and other sounds.

The Orgasm

One couple said to me, "Women don't need that part of lovemaking. All they really need is to be cuddled and made to feel like they are loved.'' Many women who are very fond of the cuddling and hugging part of lovemaking don't want to go on, possibly because they don't know what they're missing. Or there has been so much failure in this area that they've given up. They are like a mountain climber who stops short of the summit. A number of women have asked me to advise them on how to experience an orgasm. If you are one who *is* wishing you were there but can't seem to discover the secret, determine that you and your husband are going to experiment together until you do.

One thing is essential: both of you must understand the female anatomy, must find the female counterpart to the male penis on your body, the *clitoris,* and must try different ways of gently and pleasurably stimulating that organ, for it holds the key to the orgasm in a woman.

Various sexual techniques to achieve the orgasm as well as how to deal with such pleasure thieves as premature ejaculation, weak pubococcygeus muscles in the woman (a surprise to me), and psychological hindrances are well-researched in *The Act of Marriage,* by Tim and Beverly LaHaye, Zondervan Publishing House.

Oral Sex

Two of the women who read the manuscript of the book wondered if I shouldn't leave this subject out. If it offends you, skip over it. The reason I'm including it is that, in every marriage seminar we conduct, we are asked if oral sex is wrong. Many women are concerned about what is becoming a very common practice in marriage, including Christian unions. The fact that so many people ask about it makes one wonder if there isn't more than just puritanical fear involved.

We were given cause to pause one time when I received a letter from a fellow in prison who was asking what we thought about it. He said he was incarcerated because he tried to rape a girl. He couldn't help himself, he rationalized, because his wife wouldn't let him practice oral sex. It was a very flimsy excuse for rape, but what he said next intrigued me. He mentioned that the reason why she was against it was because they heard a pastor once say it was sodomy.

I looked up sodomy in the dictionary and read, first of all:

. . . the homosexual proclivities of the men of the city (Gen. 19:1-11).

Although Webster's is not divinely inspired, it is based on research and is considered accurate. It was talking, of course, about the city of Sodom which is mentioned in the Old Testament Book of Genesis. The city was destroyed with fire and brimstone because of the depravity of the people who lived there (a fact that has been corroborated by archeologists), and the greatest sin seemed to be homosexuality.

Then I read further concerning the definition of the word, and the various meanings were listed:

1. Copulation with a member of the same sex or with an animal.

2. Noncoital and esp: anal or oral copulation with a member of the opposite sex.

It doesn't mention marriage in that second description, but it certainly is talking about male and female. Some might argue that the Bible forbids sex outside the marriage bond but that within the marriage bond it is sanctioned, and since the Scriptures say "The marriage bed is undefiled," they rest their case, stating, whereas oral copulation outside marriage is a sin, within the marriage bonds there is no condemnation.

If oral sex repulses you but your husband insists upon it, you can share these thoughts with him, leaving both sides open for his consideration. If he still feels it should be a vital part of your lovemaking, you might have to readjust your thinking until his changes.

One woman who decided against it told her husband, "No more!" With that his desire increased until their sexual relationship became strained. Once she decided not to buck him on it, he didn't care to pursue it anymore.

Regarding any part of your intimate relationship, you might keep in mind what one pastor's wife wrote to me: "Couples are unwise when they pattern their sexual practices after teachings which are frequently offered by people whose own marriages have been a disaster. By following guidelines offered by the world, instead of God's way, Christians will not find His peace and satisfaction in this area.''

What's Underneath Your Lovely Locks?

Many sex problems would be solved if the lady would prepare herself for the act by setting her mind toward enjoying it. If your husband is trying to be a lover of the best variety and you're thinking about what you plan to cook for breakfast tomorrow morning, you aren't going to be able to respond, and his efforts will be irritating to you.

One lovely lady, who is married to a man many years her senior, told me that she prepares her mind for lovemaking in various ways. She enjoys amazing him with her giving of self to bring him enjoyment, since his body isn't young anymore and it is more difficult for him to play the role of lover. Among other things, she will massage his entire body with warm lotion, and while she does she will pray, "Lord, show me where to touch him to make him feel good." Then, with each stroke of the massage, she thanks God for her husband and the marriage.

When Sex Is Not His Thing

A number of women have spoken to me about their husbands who don't even *want* sex. "I'd be happy to trade with them," you might be thinking. But they're saying just the opposite.

One woman, whose husband never did want

intimacy and could see no sense in it, sighed, "I can't imagine any woman not wanting her husband to make love to her. I'd give anything if I could experience that with mine. We've made love about four times in 15 years." And yet, she would be the envy of many a woman, because her husband treats her like a queen. He adores her and will do anything for her except have sex.

If your husband isn't a real basket case in this regard, if he does show a little interest in your body, you might try what Jolene does:

> I'll tell him how attractive he is to me, how I wish I had him in my arms. Sometimes I show no interest so he'll begin to desire.

> I'll dream up unique fun things to do so lovemaking will be very interesting to him. I've learned to be patient, and he gets around to it. I just praise God that my husband wants me around all the time or I'd wonder.

At least she'll probably never have to worry about his getting interested in another woman!

Heart Check

One of the best times to make a point with a man, some women tell me, is just as your preparation for lovemaking begins, or just after lovemaking has finished. Most men are in a sugar-daddy mood then. But don't forget your basic reason for action: to lovingly help him become a better husband so HE'LL be happier, as well as you.

10

PHYSICAL ABUSE
AND ADULTERY

◆————————————————————————

Two things a bride should make clear to her husband in the beginning are: she will not tolerate physical abuse (that includes rape), and she will not tolerate his sleeping with another woman.

She needn't insult him by making it personal. When they hear of it happening to someone else, she can say, "If my husband ever hit me once, or had an affair, that would be the last time." If she says it with firm finality, nothing more needs to be said. He will get the point. If it ever happens, she needs to take fast action.

A woman who allows her husband to get away with it the first time with nothing more than an "I forgive you" is inviting him to do it again. Of course there must be forgiveness, and forgetting, but before she piously offers that pearl, she has to be sure he doesn't trample it into the mud.

I'm reminded of one very beautiful woman who came up to me after a marriage seminar in Michigan. Her husband hadn't come. She said that everything in their marriage was good, except for one thing: her husband beat her. She said, "He lays me out unconscious, and when I come to he's there on his knees, crying, washing the blood off my face very gently, and saying, 'I love you, I love you,' over and over again." Some love, huh? That guy needs a kick in the seat of his infantile temper that'll straighten him away.

The wife of an alcoholic who enjoyed things like tying her up and burning her with a cigarette lighter said to me, "I can't divorce him. I feel it's my duty as a Christian wife to stay with him. Maybe he'll turn to God and be changed." The sentiment was nice, even though it wasn't astute. Why should he turn to God? He had a football he could kick around to relieve his frustrations. She was always available when he couldn't handle life. The funny part about it was, she was a huge woman and he was a skinny little fellow. She could have whopped him across the room with one sweep of her arm, had she chosen to do so.

Insecure Females

I've discovered, in working with abused wives, that many of them are like unloved little girls. They would rather stay home and be beaten than go out and face a big wide world which might have something terrible out there for them—like someone who would beat up on them. It doesn't make sense. Or they are punishing themselves for something they've done in the past.

A young woman, married to an executive who traveled a lot, was pummeled severely every time he came home from being on the road and otherwise. Friday night seemed to be his favorite time for trying to make her into mincemeat. On one occasion his parents, brothers, and sister-in-law were there. He dragged her by the hair of her head into the bathroom, locked the door, and set about kicking and beating her so badly that she could neither stand nor sit. Then he raped her. His parents continued to watch TV, ignoring the shouting and screaming, and the bully's brother said to his own wife, who was horrified and protested to him, "It's all right. They're married."

As if that settled it! When the battered wife's mother told her that she would have called the police had she been there, the daughter said, "If you ever do that, Mom, I'll never speak to you again."

In talking with the mother, it came to light that the daughter had been extremely rebellious as a teenager, and evidently she now had a king-sized guilt complex about the way she had treated her parents during that time. It appeared as if her submission to her husband's atrocities was her way of receiving punishment she felt she deserved. I haven't heard if she's still going through her self-maintained hell or not.

It's hard to believe that some people still think a woman should accept it graciously when her husband beats up on her and should do anything he says. She is told in so many words, "Be patient while he's knocking your teeth out." Everyone who accepts *that* needs to live with a guy for awhile who has twice the strength and a hair-trigger temper that lightnings out through his fists all over *his* or *her* body, and I think we'd hear a different tune.

What Can Be Done?

Women don't like to press charges, although some women should. Their husbands are committing a crime, and it isn't showing love for the big babies by helping them continue breaking the law. Furthermore, their children are getting the idea that beating up a person weaker than themselves isn't all that serious. But some feel it doesn't do any good to call the police, or if they do and the police make an arrest, and if it should happen to be successful, they're afraid their husbands might kill them when they get out of jail.

But victims can disappear. That's what the lady did whose husband played with cigarette-lighter fire on her skin. It took her a long time to make the decision, and as I outlined a program for her, she could think of two dozen reasons why she shouldn't follow it. But she finally did. While he was out buying liquor, she grabbed what she could, caught a cab, and was gone. She had already quit her job and secured another. The next thing to do was get an apartment, which she did.

I had stressed her keeping in touch with him, letting him know that she loved him but wouldn't come back until he got his life straightened away. She called him the first time, not giving him her phone number, and then wrote him a note the next time, with no return address.

You know what happened with that fellow? The poor guy went into shock! His punching bag was gone! His toy had left. He made a beeline to the pastor of her church and began getting the help he should have gotten years before.

Before too many months had gone by, they were back together again, and the last time I heard, he was still keeping his hands off her.

If you're contemplating such a flight, remember to be prepared with the names of counselors which you can send to your husband so that while he's still in the mood, he'll head in their direction.

Adulterous Husbands

I was looking out our second-story bedroom window one morning when I noticed a pretty little female house finch trying to make time with the redheaded husband of another feathered dolly. As soon as the homemaker disappeared into the tree to put some finishing touches on the decor of her nest, the would-be homebreaker swooshed seductively to the side of the unattended male spouse, peeping her approval. In a flash, little Mrs. shot out of the branches and after the temptress.

The temptress turned tail, and then stopped and whirled around. They met beak-to-beak midair, flapping and screeching until, whooosh, the spouse had her adversary on the ground, flat on her back, wings spread wide. She had no mercy. She flopped right on top of the naughty single, tummy on tummy, wings spread just as widely. "Horrors!" I thought, "She's going to peck her to death." But she didn't. She just gave her a solid piece of her mind, did a beautiful lift-off, landed next to her husband, twittered against his bill with what looked like a, "There! You won't have to worry about *her* anymore," and went back to nest-building. The chagrined intruder wobbled through the air to a nearby perch, fluffed her feathers in embarrassed humility, and took off in the opposite direction.

I don't recommend your attacking the woman involved if your husband hasn't had sense enough to turn away. It could get you into trouble with the law, for one thing, and it could make a fool out of you, for another. One crushed wife told me she went to confront the other woman, only to find that her husband was there. It threw her into a tailspin, and she literally went into a screaming tantrum on the lawn, banging her head on the ground. She was so overcome with emotion that she lost all control. Of course it made her husband ashamed of her, and it put her out of the running altogether.

Even to confront the homebreaker means a loss of dignity for you. You should deal only with your husband, unless you think *she* thinks *he's* got money. In that case you can send word to her through someone else that he not only doesn't have much green stuff, but if she breaks up your home, you'll get at least half of it anyway, which wouldn't leave her with much to go on.

It Hurts So Much

So many emotions come to the fore when a woman finds out her husband is seeing another woman. She feels rejected, unloved, crushed, angry, and resentful, and the self-pity nearly overwhelms her. Her dreams of having a romantic, undying love from the one to whom she has given her life crashes to the floor, splintering into a thousand pieces, oftentimes never to be put together again. Many women even have the added burden of having lost the beauty of their youth, and find themselves unappealing to the few men who are out there being sought by the millions of women wanting a husband.

I've spoken with numerous women typified by one who was brought to me by a friend after I finished speaking at a women's meeting. Basically she was very pretty, but you had to look hard to realize it. Even her greeting was ground out between clenched teeth. I got right to the point: "You've allowed yourself to become bitter, hard, and ugly. Nothing is ever solved by destroying oneself."

"You'd be that way too," she spat out, "if your husband had been involved with another woman."

We talked at length, and finally I said, "You're trying to punish your husband by punishing yourself. But you're the only one who's getting hurt. It's time to let go of the hatred and reach out to God for love."

She began to cry. It was the first time the tears had flowed since her husband deceived her, she told me.

Why do women react that way? It's because of their basic emotional makeup which God gave them. Women *need* to be cherished and adored by the men to whom they've given their hearts and their bodies. A lady has to feel that her husband couldn't bear to have anyone else but her. When a husband abandons a wife for another women, he strikes at the very core of her deepest feelings. He can destroy her. She has to take special care to keep from being shattered into mental illness, extreme insecurity, or other negative emotions that render her helpless. Most of the women we have known who have come through with flying colors (after the period of anger and despair has passed) have done so by drawing their strength and power from God.

Head It Off

When lover-boy starts spending too much time talking with the pretty neighbor or a woman at work, ask him how he'd feel if you did the same thing with Bill What's-His-Name, who is a "very attractive man." Point out to him what happens to little boys who play with fire. Not only do they singe their fingers sometimes, but the fire can get out of hand and burn up the whole house.

Theresa wrote, "Before my husband was a Christian, he would go into a bar alone, and then tell me about some woman he talked with. I could tell he was tempted. I told him if he ever wanted a one-night stand, I wanted to hear all the reasons why he chose that particular woman, because if there was anything less attractive about her than me, I would be very hurt. That took the fun out, because no one compared to me in his eyes."

Beware of indulging in excessive suspicion or you'll run him right out of the house. No one can tolerate *that* for very long. Like jealousy, it destroys relationships. Reasonable trust is absolutely necessary.

If The Affair Is In Progress

Here are some things you can try:

Confront Him

Carefully. It might not be true, you know. Offhandedly mention to him that so-and-so had told you he was having an affair with someone else. Then laugh and say something like, "I told her thanks for the information, but that I didn't believe one word of it. My sweetheart knows that if he ever did, and I found out about it, it could end what has been a beautiful relationship—not perfect, but beautiful. Besides, he loves his children and he wouldn't want to lose them (or if older, their respect)." Then drop it.

If he confesses, or continues, come on strong. Be sure you are calm enough so you don't burst out crying or lose control. You may show a quiet, holy anger without sinning. Let him know that you are aware of what he is doing, and if he values your marriage, he'll back out immediately. Be prepared with a written sheet, pointing out all the losses he will suffer if he lets it go on so it destroys your life together. Compare them with the few gains he would make.

Explain that he is experiencing erotic love, which is pure physical attraction (chemistry) and which will undoubtedly cool after awhile because it is not based on solid ground. Point out that it would be foolish indeed to destroy the higher level of love which, though not perfect, has resulted from years of sharing between you.

Go on to assure him that you will try to be a better, more exciting wife (of course you won't accept all the blame for his transgression), but until you are certain he has quit this nonsense, he will not touch you physically, and he isn't to expect you to do much but be cool toward him. Furthermore, you expect him to quit it now.

If he wants time, give it to him, but set a date on it—perhaps two days—so the other woman won't have a chance to talk him into doing something rash. Make it clear that you expect him to tell her that he loves his wife the most, that he doesn't want the family to break up, that everything is over—and not to get in touch with him again. Keep yourself as alluring and gorgeous as possible so that he'll want to end it all and get back to your bed.

The Disappearing Act

Like abusive husbands, one thing that most of the male species can't bear is to have their wives walk out on them. So if he doesn't break his affair off, disappear with your children, and don't let him know where you are for a few days. Then contact him by phone to see how he's reacting. This time, if he says he'll end the affair, have the agreement that he will do it over the phone (with you listening) and then get counseling.

It's only fair to warn you that you do take a chance of his not wanting you to come back, but you're taking the chance of losing him anyway. A woman who just sits around letting it happen, when her husband *knows* she knows, loses his respect.

After we had spoken at a meeting in New York, a tremulous, attractive woman shared her sorrow with me. Her husband had a mistress. For years he had been dividing his time between the two women. He'd spend three months with his wife, then three months with his mistress.

I asked, "Why do you put with this?"

"Well," she replied, "I don't want to lose him, and if I walked out he'd just go to her."

"Really?" I queried. "He goes to her anyway, doesn't he? Have you considered disappearing?"

As she started recalling, she remembered a time when the mistress got fed up and took off to parts unknown. She said her husband nearly went crazy. He searched all over the country until he found her and brought her back so he could continue his double life.

Living with a man like that would be as palatable as eating unripened persimmons eight times a day. Not only did her husband need professional counseling to see why he had never been able to grow up, but she needed the same to find out why in the world she'd settle for such a silly arrangement.

Wait It Out

Since I've said you must nip such behavior in the bud immediately, it may seem strange that I am now suggesting that you wait it out. I'm not sure that I could myself. But many woman have, and successfully, so I'm passing it on to you. If this is your husband's first indiscretion, it may be his last. If you let your pride shut him out of your life, he may be forced into divorce, and you will spend years regretting it after his passion for the other woman has cooled.

If you decide on this course of action, don't let him know you know. The affair may last only a short period of time. Be especially charming when he is home. Let him know about the guys who flirt with you downtown. Get some hobbies, so you'll have new subjects to talk about. Change your hairdo often, as well as your makeup, and get some new clothes, even if he hollers about the bills. After all, he's spending some fun money on her.

If you have some information about someone who had an affair, lost his mate, and loused up his life as well as that of his children, share it with him.

When the affair is over, tell him you knew all the time, that you said nothing because you realized that you could be tempted too, but that you would never put up with it a second time.

Then forgive and forget, not bringing it up again.

One woman who told me she waited it out confessed that their marriage is now stronger than ever before. The affair forced her to face up to some correcting in her own life that needed to be done.

The Chronic Offender

One little wife who contacted me by long-distance phone had five children whom her husband had fathered between his extracurricular affairs. His latest flame came home with him, and the two of them berated the wife for "condemning" them. They weren't doing anything wrong, they declared. "We're just as good Christians as you are," the mistress declared. They even had the gall to tell her she was the only one sinning because she was judging them. The one encounter turned into several encounters, each ugly and bitter.

Submitting to her husband's sexual advances time and again, even though she knew he was having affairs, caused her to be saddled with a houseful of children, no money, and a jail she couldn't break out of. There was little I could tell her to do, except to start educating herself so she could get a job to support the children later (perhaps taking a correspondence course) should he walk out permanently. I suggested that she start making herself as attractive as possible but not to be available physically to him until his life changed.

I passed on one more piece of advice. I suggested that she get involved with praying friends who could turn the power on in behalf of her husband. I've seen worse people do an about-face when God got hold of their lives.

If You Are The Adulteress

So often we're told, "To have a happy marriage, you must be honest with your mate about everything." Honesty is equated with telling all you know. If you had an affair and it is over, why saddle your mate with the heartache of knowing that you did? If you have stopped it and have truly repented, confessing it as a sin to God, it is forgiven and forgotten by God if you are His child. I wouldn't suggest tempting the Almighty again, however. Next time He just might let you learn the hard way by bearing the consequences. But your husband would never be able to forget, and possibly not forgive, either. It might also drive him to an affair himself.

Rather, be busy correcting yourself and helping your husband to correct anything either of you might be doing to bring that type of temptation into your life.

Heart Check

If you are smoldering with hatred or melting with compliance to anything your husband insists on, your heart is not right. For your sake, as well as his, you must avoid such extremes so that you can stay healthy and strong and meet your problem maturely.

11

WHERE DID
MR. FIX-IT GO?

The mockingbird is one of the wonders of the world, in my estimation. Sleek, beautifully marked when flying, with flashes of white accenting the dark gray, this delightful creation of God entertains us several months out of the year with almost-continual song. We have listened for an hour at a stretch in amazement as each phrase he warbles seems to be a new, inventive approach to musical composition. Can you imagine his female counterpart not adoring his serenade? I know of one that didn't.

An elderly friend of mine told me of watching a male mocker entertaining the world with his song. All at once his mate came zooming out of her nesting area and pecked him soundly over and over again on his head. After having made certain he would quit his clamor and joymaking while she had the job of sitting on their eggs, she went back to her task, satisfied that she had taught him some responsibility.

I wouldn't recommend the same surprise for your hubby, but you can get his attention in a perfectly acceptable way.

It's an age-old story, but true, and plenty of women are continuing to growl about it: "My husband won't fix things around the house." "Mr. King relaxes each evening while I work on and on." "My man won't help. He expects me to do everything." "We both work during the day outside the home, but when evening comes, guess who has to do all the housework and take care of the children? I do. His lordship won't lift a hand."

Same Song, Second Verse

At a retreat where I was the speaker, I asked the women to share with me what they did to encourage hubby to be the kind of man that causes a little boy to say, "My dad can do anything!"

Lorene, with 42 years of marriage behind her, stated flatly, "He's a man. What more can I say? I don't mind (most of the time anyway) because the alternative I would mind very much."

Another response was, "I do nothing. I can put up with his not helping with the kids or doing the yardwork."

But there are many who think differently. If your muscle man is not pulling his share of the load when it comes to keeping up the home, you'll want to consider some of the solutions that have worked with others.

As you get into practical applications, pave your way with rubies by keeping these basic principles in mind:

1) Utilize the methods of approach and communication discussed in the earlier chapters before you attempt to move Mr. Do Little to do more.

2) If you know he has a real hangup about some type of chore, don't ask him to do *that* one until he has learned that it's *fun* pleasing you.

3) Neither should you ask him to do something you know he is not capable of doing. He will just get discouraged and be much harder to move next time. After all, there are challenges you don't meet so well either, aren't there?

4) When you need a reluctant husband to tackle what he considers a mountain, suggest that he do only part of what you want, instead of the whole rock heap. You can suggest another portion of the project on another day.

5) Let him choose his *time* preference for doing any certain chore, suggesting a couple of alternatives. For instance, "Would Friday after work or Saturday morning be best for you?"

6) Keep a sense of humor and a pleasant manner.

7) Compliment him warmly and thank him for each task he does, no matter how insignificant. Point out his strengths. Say things like, "You can do practically anything, can't you?" with an admiring look in your eyes. If you say it long enough he'll begin to see the truth of it, and you'll see activity pick up.

8) Keep up your end of the homework. Have your house clean and neat. If you must have extra shelves to keep it that way, get them. Consider selling, throwing, or giving away items that you haven't used for five years.

9) Some men figure that women do

nothing all day anyway, and they're *sure* of it if they come home to a TV blaring away. Without a doubt it's a time-waster and a slower-downer even when you are doing a chore in front of it. If you feel you must watch it, turn it off before he walks in the door.

Making Work Fun!

It's not impossible to turn work into recreation. My husband proved this with our youngsters. Every Saturday since they were little, he has made out a list entitled "Our Fun Day in the Sun List," "Today's Happy Times Together List," or something similar. One time we were both away on a speaking tour, so our teenage children were home alone. They went ahead without us on "workday." Our daughter cleaned the house and garage to surprise us, and our son worked on the yard. He had made out a list for himself entitled, "My Fun Day in the Sun Even Though Dad Isn't Here to Enjoy It With Me List."

Many men like some version of the list idea. Some women label them "Honey Do List" or "Job Jar." I especially like one lady's title: "Things to Do Because You Love Me." The wife jots chores down on a piece of paper every week, which she tapes to the refrigerator, or on several pieces of paper, which are dropped into a jar or basket. As each item is taken care of, it is scratched off the list or the paper is destroyed.

Chad wrote, "My wife will say, 'Honey, I've prayed about the chores I've put on this piece of paper. So you are responsible to God regarding what you do with them.' It really gets me going because I feel I have to answer to Him for my actions."

Several families wrote that they gather weekly around a list and each individual decides which items on the list he or she can do. Dad might say, "I'll oil the hinges, trim the trees, dig the hole, touch up the paint on the woodwork, and change the oil in the car." Teenage son decides he can mulch the garden, mow the lawns, and water the bushes. Ten-year-old daughter wants to wash the dog, weed the flower bed, and make cookies. Tiny brother cleans out his toy chest. Mother concentrates on the rest.

Some families prefer to tackle some of the chores together so they can chat, sing, and share while they're at it.

If The Big Weekly
Gets Small Response

Even if you get nothing but a yawn should you suggest any of the preceding, you can lighten your daily workload by encouraging your king to do half.

Cassandra's husband is no go-getter when it comes to yardwork or housework. She handles it by getting all cutied up in some work clothes and starting a job, like weeding the garden. Then she'll come to him and say pleasantly, "Why don't you come join me? It'll be fun doing it together." If it's vacuuming, she'll say, "Honey, would you mind doing a little of this heavy pushing? Just a minute. I'll move this chair. It's . . . unnh! . . . in . . . the way . . .unnh- . . . whew! I guess I need your strong back for this, too." Or another day she issues the invitation, "Let's wash the car together, shall we?"

Whatever it is, while they work together, she tells him interesting things, brings him a cold drink, and generally makes it pleasurable for him.

A good idea was shared by Christy: "After Daddy gets home and before anybody can eat dinner, everything that's out of place in the house must be put away by the person who left it out. We work hard at it and it really helps."

A real timesaver is: when your husband gets up to go into another room, hand him something that's out of place and smile, "Darling, would you mind taking this with you?"

Or put his idle fingers to work while his eyes are glued to the day's prime-time program. Along with "Honey, would you mind . . . ?" hand him a bowl of nuts to crack, silver to polish, or cherries to pit for the pie you're making for his watering mouth.

Dorene's husband always took his socks off, peeling them from the top down so they were inside-out when she went to wash them—an irritation to her. No amount of pleading with him changed that habit. Then she hit upon an idea. While he was watching the boob tube, she cooed, "Sweetie, while you're watching, will you put these into pairs?" As he did so, he had to turn them right-side-out, and he began to see what she had been complaining about. Now he remembers to do it when he takes them off. The only problem now, she says, is that he sometimes mismatches the socks and goes to work with two different ones on. They haven't solved that one yet.

Speaking of Socks

A pastor's wife whose husband would just . . . drop . . . his dirty socks on the bedroom floor for her to pick up, finally (after first asking and then enjoining him with no results), started shoving them under the bed, out of sight, with her foot. The day came when he didn't have any socks of the right color.

"Where are my socks?" he asked.

"Oh! Well, Dear, I found them on the floor! They didn't look good there, so I . . . (leaning over and lifting the bed cover) . . . pushed them under here . . . see?"

"But they're dirty!"

"I'll wash them for you. Just drop them in the laundry basket next time you're going by."

With that she cheerily left the room. It worked, and her husband laughingly tells it on himself.

A favorite solution for dropped dirty socks came in my mail. Lisa's Terrance was a great one for ignoring her pleas concerning the problem. She talked it over with him calmly. No change. She bawled him out angrily. He just laughed. She appealed to his sense of manhood. He was unimpressed.

"The trouble with you," a friend advised, "is that you are forgetting your role as a submissive, loving wife. You should be picking up the socks yourself with a cheerful attitude."

But Lisa couldn't quite swallow the idea of encouraging her husband's immature behavior, so she had a think time with herself and decided to try one other approach. Since every man has a lot of the little boy in him, she reasoned, maybe an appeal to that part of his nature might do the trick. The result was a basketball hoop, handmade, and placed over a receptacle. He thought it was great to *sink* the wadded-up socks in as few tries as possible.

And Other Things

Troila contributed, "My husband would leave newspapers and magazines he read on the floor, or his tools where he had been working. Anything he used, it seems, was never put away. At first I picked up for him, because my asking did no good. But at last I decided just to leave his items where he left them. I kept the rest of the house neat, and it was embarrassing to me when friends dropped over and saw a pile of tools in the middle of the room, but I resisted doing his job. After some time of walking around the piles, he eventually began to understand that his participation was important."

Unfinished Jobs

If the problem is a starter who never finishes, keep an eye on him, and when he begins to tire of what he is doing, move quickly to his side, saying, "Here, Honey, I'll help you finish." If he protests, you can add, "There is so much on our schedule that I know we'll never get back to it. We'd better finish now while we have an opportunity." If he does go along with it, comment afterward, "Doesn't it make you feel good to have it all done?" After a few years of this, he just may do it on his own.

The Irresistible Ploy

One fellow wrote, "At times my wife speeds me up by trying, in the usual incompetent female manner, to do things she is incapable of doing. When this happens, I usually rise to the bait." Forget his description of our gender. She gets him to do it, doesn't she? A wife who is all thumbs, with a cut or two on the hand and a messy completed job, just might convince him that he has certain capabilities you don't. No fair *pretending* unless he knows you are kidding around. Dishonesty has a way of backfiring.

You may be able to do more than you think. George always has done the yard work faithfully, at least as much as he is able to squeeze in on Saturdays and on some evenings. Lately, though, I've been spending an hour or two on as many mornings as possible in shoveling, picking and transporting dirt, encouraging sad plants, and sinking bulbs into the ground, because it is such marvelous exercise and infinitely more interesting than doing bends and situps. Perhaps it would be to your advantage to do some of those chores yourself (see Chapter 4).

Stronger Action

Polly complained that her husband gets involved with expensive, time-consuming projects which keep him from doing things which are very important and needful for her. ("He knows I've wanted improvements in my kitchen for five years.") Her husband said,

She finally detailed everything she

wanted on paper, including new appliances, carpentering, painting. Then the price estimates came next, on all of it, and how long it would take to get it done. When she showed it to me, explaining her intentions and the costs involved, if we hired help, I realized how important it was to her, and that it wouldn't be out of reach financially. So I gave her the go-ahead to hire some of the help and was able to do some of it myself.

Perry's wife handled it this way:

She wanted a big window put in our master bedroom. It seemed like a lot of work to me, and I just couldn't see that it would make that much difference in the looks of the room. One day she came home with a window the size she wanted under her arm, presented it to me with a smile and a kiss and flattered me into believing that I could do it better than a professional carpenter she was planning to hire. I did it, and I have to admit, the room looks much nicer.

You may have to take a stronger step, which is another variation of the foregoing. Let's say you want a screen door fixed that's not hanging straight, and he just never seems to get to it. Your line: "I've hired a fellow to come out to fix that. He'll be here tomorrow (don't fib—be sure you've called him). It'll cost us about (?). He probably can't do it as well as you can, but it'll save you having to do it. And I just can't stand it like that any longer." Maybe he'll just tell you to cancel the fellow so he can do it himself.

If those ideas don't work, you may have to go

one point stronger. Wait six months and then hire someone to do it with no warning ahead of time. When your reluctant partner gets the bill, he may decide it would be wise if he stirred himself a bit. You can purr, "Sweetie, I knew you didn't want to be bothered and we really had to have it done. We'll pay it off somehow. We can always scrimp a little on the grocery bill."

All Tuckered Out?

Your husband may be too bushed to want to do anything around home. His health may not be up to par, and the cause may originate in your kitchen. Happily, the public is becoming aware of the debilitating effects that such items as white flour, sugar, and stimulants such as coffee have on the body.

Check into the possibility that your man may have low blood sugar (hypoglycemia). Call around until you find a doctor who treats it. Your health food store ought to know of someone in your area, or look in your yellow pages for an M.D. who is listed under preventive or nutritional medicine.

Another exciting procedure to explore is the use of chelation therapy, which is a nonsurgical method of cleansing the arteries of plaque and undesirable metals. It is enjoying tremendous success in preventing heart attacks and strokes, and is healing victims of those diseases. The number of doctors who use chelation therapy is increasing, but some states have only a few. For detailed information about chelation, read *Supernutrition for Healthy Hearts* by Dr. Richard Passwater published by the Dial Press,

New York, New York, 10017. If you are interested in finding out who does chelation
where you live, write to A.A.M.P., (American
Academy of Medical Preventics), 8383 Wilshire
Blvd, Suite 922, Beverly Hills, California 90211
and request a booklet giving the names and ad-
dresses of those doctors.

Back To The Finches

This spring several pairs of house finches
decided to build in some tall trees which accent
the front of our home. Their joy was infectious.
The male seemed to do nothing as far as manual
labor was concerned in gathering material for
the nest or in building their future home. But he
was superb at the romance bit. He would chirp,
flit, and encourage, selecting a branch on which
to sit while his mate took her treasures (a string,
a piece of plant, etc.) into the tree to create a
nesting spot for her babies. As soon as she came
out of the tree he would be by her side, chirping
his approval as she selected her materials and
went aloft with them.

Heart Check

*Perhaps your fella is like the finch.
He's so romantic that you don't CARE
if he helps or not. If that's the funniest
thing you've heard all week, at least consider
this: is there a possibility that he has been doing
SOME helping around the home—or he used to
—that you aren't or weren't noticing? Being
aware of the efforts he does make and com-
plimenting him for them will help you be more
understanding as you wait for other improvements to come.*

12

MONEY AND TENSIONS GO HAND-IN-HAND

The love of money and the desire to control its use seem to have the same effect in many marriages as ice cream touching an exposed nerve in a tooth. "Togetherness" and "partner-ship" are loving terms that might apply anywhere but around the paycheck. Lovers can become enemies in a hurry if one of the two doesn't give up almost total rights to deciding how and when their funds should be spent. Although women can be just as much the cause of this difficulty as men, the fact that the male has traditionally been "boss" over money matters does seem to put the biggest share of the problem in the wives' laps.

Not Hamburger Again!

Oftentimes we're confronted with complaints from a person who bemoans the fact that her mate simply has no sense when it comes to spending money, and doesn't want to budget.

If that rings a bell at your house, you might try what Elizabeth did. Her professional husband had no interest in spending money wisely (a hint of her difficulty was in Chapter 1). Quietly, each month, she would ask that they discuss the funds as they came in. With the paycheck in front of them, she would ask, "Do you intend to buy something for your boat again?" If he did, and it cut sharply into their income, she simply served him ground beef for a week. She said she was careful never to do it bitterly, but cheerfully, and when he complained, she would say, "Oh, don't worry, Dear, I can put up with it. I want you to have that item for your boat, so we had to sacrifice somewhere." Needless to say, that kept his spending under some control.

She Had To Cry

Eunice was humiliated one day when she tried to charge a shirt for their son in a large department store. Suddenly the store manager appeared and rudely yanked her credit card out of her hand. She said she had never wanted a big black hole to open underneath her as badly as she did that day. Her husband had been at it again. He had charged $1500 for a bedroom set when they had no money!

Somehow she had been able to cover for his blunders before, but now she felt she had come to the end of her strength. Once at home, she cried and cried. When her husband came home, she told him what had happened, and said, "I can't handle it anymore."

From that time on, he turned the money and the credit cards over to her. They have an agreement now that he spends nothing until she's had a chance to check the budget to see if they can afford it.

If your babe has weaknesses in this area, you can have your conference (remember— right time, right place, right approach as discussed in preceding chapters), and lovingly, kindly give this a go:

Honey, you have some marvelous strengths that I don't have. (Then name some.) I admire you so much. I'm glad you aren't perfect, though, because I'm so imperfect. That's what's so beautiful about our marriage. We balance each other out. Where I'm weak, you're strong. Where you're weak, I'm strong. Now, about the budgeting. (You can have an affectionate "heh heh" ready to to go here.) It just isn't your thing, I'm beginning to realize, and it's unfair of me to expect you to fit into a slot that isn't your kind of slot. Why don't I try doing the spending for us for awhile? I won't do anything without your approval, except make us all stick to the budget, so we can get out of debt and get on with that dream we have."

By keeping the funds out of his hands, you might be able to get ahead.

The Cheater

Patsy said it used to be her job to pay all the bills. It got pretty tiresome for her, though, because Ron continually accused her of cheating him. So she decided to take drastic action. She went to work outside the home to supplement their income and so she would have some spending money. That put him in the position of paying the bills a couple of times. Was he in for a shock! His wife hadn't been cheating him at all! The economy was the culprit. Now they pay the bills and go shopping together.

The Goose Shocked The Gander

Likewise, Leina's Perry was excellent at

spending money on things he enjoyed, but he refused to let her have any. She had a surprise awaiting him one day. She had gone out and gotten a job. And guess what she did with her first paycheck. That's right—she spent it *all* on herself—every penny of it. She bought things she'd been wanting for years. He didn't like it *at all,* and soon called for a little talk. He thought, he said, that it would be nice if they pooled their money and made decisions on how they should spend it— together. The problem was solved.

When He Says No To Nice Things

Some men see absolutely no sense in buying furniture other than what you acquired 32 years ago from grandmother's attic or the Salvation Army. They think pretty clothes are foolish, even though they may admire other women who wear them. They may consider flowers, even the ones you plant, a total waste of money, and as for "romantic" gifts, forget it! You're more likely to receive a pancake turner for Christmas.

If the item you need to keep you a prettier, happier wife so he will always be a contented-to-stay-home-with-you-husband is affordable within the family budget, whether you've earned the money yourself or not, consider what Clarice shared:

> I've learned in some areas not to ask. When I feel we need something for the house, for instance, I buy it. Once it's in its place, he seldom says anything.

Maybe *you* are the culprit. Some women have

run their mates right out of the house because they were such penny-pinchers. Delia confessed, "I was so conservative I wouldn't even buy myself some lovely underthings so I could make our sexual life exciting." Her husband remarried years ago, but she has not.

Whoever Handles It Best

Many men and women go into marriage with the idea that women just can't be trusted with handling money. Generally it's nothing but a cultural hand-me-down. If you can put yourself in a position where you can prove to your husband that you are capable, sensible, and really quite intelligent, you can make it clear that you wish to have more say in financial matters in your house and even handle certain of the funds yourself.

Budgeting, spending, and savings should, ideally, be a togetherness thing, with the one in charge who is strongest in the handling of it. No adult, including you, should be treated like a little child who begs for handouts. You should have some spending money for which you don't have to account to him. However, if you *act* like a little child by abusing your credit card privileges, spending every cent you get your eager hands on, and not doing comparative buying, then most certainly you should take yourself in hand very firmly. With your husband's help, set some restrictive guidelines and goals, cut up your credit cards, and learn your financial ABC's before you go any further.

Mr. Rockefeller

It's said that the original super-rich

Rockefeller taught his children to give the first 10 percent of their wages to the Lord, the second 10 percent to others, and the third 10 percent to savings. Only then should they spend anything for themselves.

That's not a bad idea as long as you hold the remaining 70 percent to the line. My husband often says that many of his millionaire clients are that way because they *don't* spend their money. In one very real sense it's true. Many of them sacrificed and did without for years in order to get ahead. Nor is it unusual for people in that bracket to spend practically nothing in comparison with what they have, whereas people who have no savings or investments are great at buying whatever their hearts desire.

One family, whose papa makes $2,500 a month, is $15,000 in debt. Creditors are continually turning their accounts over to credit bureaus, and the embarrassment and unhappiness that results causes almost constant squabbling between the parents, with each pointing the finger of blame at the other.

They seem most willing to do anything you suggest. I've sat with them, helped them work out a budget and a spending program, and they've agreed that it is indeed a grand scheme. They'll do it, I'm assured each time. And then the following week one of their children will mention casually that they've just bought a new horse, are going to fly down to Disneyland for a vacation (because they didn't have time on the vacation which they took two months before), or that they all started piano lessons yesterday. They send their children to expensive private schools, and the father takes their family of six out to dinner once a week.

At home they stock up on candy, white flour and sugar, pastries, expensive frozen foods and canned goods, and wonder why they are continually ill.

Characteristic of almost every person whom my husband and I have tried to help get on their feet by giving them or loaning them funds is that very often the dollars received to pay the rent or buy the equipment needed to get started in a little business are spent on dinners in a restaurant, expensive foods at the grocery store, furniture they could have done without, and a host of other "necessities."

Hold That Line!

So many couples complain to us, "There just isn't enough money to go around." What they generally mean is, "We don't have enough for the luxuries we want." If you learn to do without the smaller things now, you will be able to save for the bigger ones, and the little ones will follow later. It's nice to have all the new appliances and gadgets that come on the market. It's nice to have pool tables and the latest Frisbees. But those items aren't necessary for your survival.

Your children can do without some of the things their playmates have. If you give them too much now, you take away much of the joy they can have in working toward their own goals. They don't need their own swimming pool, whether on top of the ground or in it. They even can do without a bicycle (unless they need it for a job or transportation to a school that's far away). It was just two generations ago that many little people didn't have all the things considered necessities for children today. That generation had some built-in values about what is important in life that are often lacking in today's youngsters who continually want, want, and want more, never being satisfied with what they have.

We have friends who lived under Communist rule in China until just recently. Since most of their material goods were taken away from them, they learned to live very simply. Now that they are in the United States, they will say to their grown children, "We have food. We need nothing more. Don't work so hard. Enjoy our family." There is much to what they say. They found that some things aren't as important as they once thought, and much of what they once considered essential wasn't.

Budgeting In Your Dreams

One young couple desperately wanted a house. They had lived in a small apartment for the first 12 years of their marriage, and since they had adopted two children, they felt they needed more room and a better environment for them. They hadn't saved a penny during those 12 years. Although they were making average wages between them, they had so many "necessities" that they considered themselves poor. The "necessities" were concerts they *had* to attend, weekend vacations they needed, eating out frequently, and similar activities. They hounded their parents for a down payment to a house, but the parents wisely refused.

Finally the father confronted them with the fact that if they would get busy and save half the down payment for a house, he would *lend* them the other half and they could pay it back on a monthly basis, interest-free. That couple, who couldn't find an extra penny at the end of each month, had their half of the down payment saved within an eight-month period! They were amazed. Their parents were amazed. Everybody was amazed at what they could do once they set their minds to doing it. They learned to trim and deny. As a result, today they're settled in a nice little home that has increased much in value since they purchased it.

Insurance And A Will

All good budgets should include more than a dream of the future. They should be realistic about the future. There are two items that ought to be in everyone's thinking, even if it means you have to sell your TV to get them: life insurance and a will. Because we covered the necessities of both and the why's and wherefore's of what is involved in acquiring both in our book *Successful Financial Planning,* I won't try to duplicate that information now.

Suffice it to say that George has had many weeping widows in his law office over the years because their husbands had died, leaving them with inadequate insurance or no will, and they find themselves faced with ominous mountains that they cannot climb.

Don't let it happen to you. If your husband hasn't apprised you of all the facts concerning your family business affairs, take it upon yourself to find out about them, no matter how distasteful the whole idea might seem to you.

Become Knowledgeable

Visualize a future without your husband, figuring out what it would cost you to maintain your present standard of living for you and your children (if you have any) and, considering inflation, what amount of capital you would need to supply future needs. Figure what you would need to keep you home caring for them rather than turning them over to someone else.

After you have come up with a fairly good estimate, call some insurance agents to get facts about policies available. You might wish to consider low-cost term insurance, which 'with very reasonable rates' could swell your estate overnight to a size that would take care of all your economic needs should you suddenly become a widow.

Present your concerns, and all the information, to your husband. Stand firm on this need. It is a necessary protection.

Then, as quickly as you can get to an attorney's office, get a will made, including a proper trust, if necessary, to care for your children. Choose an estate-planning expert who can figure out the best ways to help your estate save taxes, if needed. Arrange for the care of your children in the event of the death of both of you.

If you don't have a will made, be aware of the fact that the state will make the decisions concerning all your goods and your children should you pass from this scene, and the results may not be at all what you would have wanted. The people you would want for guardians may not be whom the judge decides on at all. Impress this upon your husband. The sooner you get it done the better. You never know when your time here is finished. George has dealt with the affairs of a number of children whose young parents have both been taken suddenly.

Even if children aren't involved, you need a will. My George has been able to help widows save hundreds of thousands of dollars in their estates through tax savings just by wording the will properly. He's been able to turn over millions to God's work that would ordinarily have gone to taxes or to distant relatives who cared little for the deceased. He's been able to keep many loved ones from squandering money on foolish things simply by setting up a proper trust for the person who would receive the funds.

See your attorney. It's one of the best investments you can ever make.

The Worrier

If you worry about money, perhaps you need a fresh perspective regarding it. Actually everything we own belongs to God anyway— not to us. He asks that we return 10 percent of it to Him to be given directly to His work (churches, missions, etc.), allowing us to make the decisions regarding the rest. If He's the One who is really in charge in your life, then why are you concerned? If your spending is done with serving Him in mind rather than just for your own pleasure, He won't snatch it away from you.

If you have been faithful in money matters with Him, and you still aren't exactly well off, then He has put you in that position for a reason—perhaps so you can relate to others in the same economic bracket.

Heart Check

Whether you have or haven't surrendered your life to the Lord, there is another consideration. When Jesus was tempted by the devil at the beginning of His ministry, the evil one offered to give Him the world's kingdoms if Jesus would fall down and worship him. That's because God has given this wicked one temporary charge of the world and all the wealth that's in it. He's been clever enough to lead a lot of people straight to his lair with a promise of gold beyond their wildest dreams. But of course Jesus refused this offer. Be careful that you don't choose to follow the wrong god. The testimonies of many multimillionaires who were miserable up to their death, despite their wealth, should convince you that there's something better out there, somewhere. If you want to find out what, read on. There's good news awaiting you.

13

STEP FIVE—IT
WORKS EVERY TIME!

◆───────────────────────

We have seen that your husband's failure to supply your needs actually becomes a terrific weakness in his life. We also have discovered that it is your God-given responsibility to communicate those needs to the love of your life through words, action, and attitudes.

If you have followed God's directions in that regard, and nothing has changed, don't worry. There's another step you can take to help that reluctant husband come around that works every time! You have a pot of gold you haven't even found yet! And its value is guaranteed not to dip with the economy. That gold is a promise held out to you by your heavenly Father, who loves you and wants the best for you, and it's expressed in this Bible verse: ASK WHAT YOU WILL, AND IT SHALL BE DONE UNTO YOU.

If you are one of those who have asked, asked, and asked again, and the dream didn't come true, it may be because you didn't understand that there is a condition attached to that promise. Let's read that verse again, in its entirety:

IF YOU ABIDE IN ME, AND MY WORDS ABIDE IN YOU, YOU SHALL ASK WHAT YOU WILL, AND IT SHALL BE DONE UNTO YOU.

That certainly does color the rainbow a bit differently, doesn't it? Abiding in Christ is like abiding in your home. Your home surrounds you when you are there, doesn't it? Every room influences your thinking and helps determine your actions. When you are in your kitchen, your mind turns to meal preparation, or eating. When you are in the bedroom, you think of sleep or preparing your body for the day's activities. You do many things in your home that you wouldn't do elsewhere.

So we are to abide in Jesus, allowing Him to surround us, influencing our thinking on all matters. We are to talk, walk, and plan with Him, as we let His words sink into our hearts and minds. We study it. We memorize it. We use it. We obey it.

Naughties We Do

When we sin, we are obviously not abiding in Jesus. To get back on the track, we must admit each sin to God, and the sooner the better, just as we apologize to a mate when we have offended. If we fail to admit our sins, our communication lines to God are short-circuited. We don't lose our place in His family, any more than a child of yours is no longer your child when he disobeys you, but we won't see a whole lot of our prayers answered, and the joy of being a Christian isn't there. The minute we admit our wrong to God, however, with the sincere intent of turning our backs on that sin, He lovingly and cheerfully is wide open to us again, and once again we are abiding. If we wish our prayers to be answered, then, we need to keep "fessed up."

IF WE CONFESS OUR SINS, HE IS FAITHFUL AND JUST TO FORGIVE US OUR SINS

AND TO CLEANSE US FROM ALL UNRIGHTEOUSNESS.

Abiding Isn't All

When our family vacationed in Hawaii, we ministered in a church whose membership was almost entirely former Buddhists who had converted to Christianity. While I was interviewing some of those women for radio, they told me that they used to have family altars in their homes. Presiding over the altar was an idol—a statue of Buddha or perhaps a ceramic cat. To please their god, they brought sacrifices of rice, fruit, or other things to lay on that altar.

We have been asked to bring a sacrifice too—the sacrifice of *praise,* and it's to be brought to the living God all the time, accompanied by thank you's.

One day I suggested to a little wife that she try praising God for everything continally, instead of repeating her requests over and over again, and then perhaps she would see answers to prayer. She said, "Nowhere in the Bible does it say we are to praise continually. That's not real."

I answered, "Want me to quote a Scripture to you on that?" With her "Yes," I shared,

LET US OFFER THE SACRIFICE OF PRAISE TO GOD CONTINUALLY, THAT IS, THE FRUIT OF OUR LIPS GIVING THANKS TO HIS NAME.

She said, "It's hard." I agreed. That's why our understanding God calls it a sacrifice. The harder a situation seems, the harder it is to make your lips praise and say, "Thank You!"

But when you force your lips to do so, the heart will soon follow, and the pot will tip over to pour heavenly gold right into your life. Prayers are answered, sometimes miraculously! Problems untangle beautifully. If God doesn't answer the way you feel He should, He will show you His blessing in the answer He does give.

She Did What Came Naturally

My friend, Samantha, is a classic example of how powerfully praise and thanks work with a husband and others. She was at the point of desperation as her second marriage was in danger of crumbling and her eldest son was into heavy drugs.

Someone cared enough to invite her to a prayer meeting. Never having attended anything *that* radical, she was sure the ladies there were absolutely crazy. But she was intrigued, and returned. Before many more meetings, she invited Jesus Christ to take charge of her broken life, and, absolutely characteristic of Him, He started doing so.

She was so overwhelmed with the release and relief that her new Master had brought to her that she began to praise and thank Him as she had heard the ladies in the prayer meeting do. For everything! The grass that was greener than yesterday. The flowers that were more fragrant. The fact that He was able to handle the problems in her life that she had tried so long to conquer.

She wanted her huband to experience her newfound joy too, but since she had destroyed one marriage because she didn't communicate correctly, she hesitated to do more than share very cautiously with him about what had happened to her. But she could do one thing with all her might: praise! So every time she thought of Roger, she began to praise and thank God for what *He* was going to do with him. Every time she thought of her sons she praised God and thanked Him for what He was going to do with them.

When the eldest son would come home from school and fall on the floor, spaced out on drugs, she would cover him with a blanket and say, "Oh, Honey, you're such a wonderful boy. God is going to do something beautiful in your life someday." *(What would you say to YOUR teenager in a case like that, hmmmmm?)* He'd curse her and tell her to get out of the room. She would, but once outside the door, she'd begin to quietly praise and thank God again for what He was going to do with her son.

Did God do anything? Did He ever! With her whole family! Three months after she started praising, her husband decided to give up a habit he had—smoking dope.

Before the year was out, her youngest son, who went with his mother to "some of those weird prayer meetings," as he put it, became a Christian.

By the time a year of praising and thanking had gone by, the eldest son decided to quit drugs totally, and he did.

A year later her husband came to Jesus for love and salvation.

Four years after she had surrendered her life to her Creator, Samantha came rushing over to my house, jumped out of her car, and passed on the sweetest news she could give me. Her eldest son had just prayed to receive Jesus, and she had the privilege of being the one who prayed with him!

As I was reading this portion of the manuscript of this book to her to check the story for accuracy, she began to laugh. "You haven't heard the latest," she said. "My sister and youngest brother came to the Lord just two months ago, while I was visiting them, and just the day before yesterday my eldest brother called. In the course of the conversation he said, 'Nothing would thrill me more than to have the Lord come in to take over my life.' " Her reaction was a surprised but joyful exclamation, and together they prayed over the telephone while he walked from darkness into light.

Does it work? Is the sun in the sky? Is water wet?

When you've tried everything the Lord has asked you to do as a wife and you don't get results, if you are "abiding" and the communication lines to your heavenly Father are open, you can turn the problem over to Him, lock, stock, and store, and expect Him to take care of the matter for you. Praise and thanks become continual in your life.

But HOLD ON! There's an important question you must answer before you start your sacrificial praise and thanks and can expect God to listen:

Are You In The Right Camp?

Queen Esther, whose life we explored in the early chapters of this book, was in the right place at the right time. She was one of God's own people, so she could call upon His help when she needed it. How often I've heard testimonies of women like Edith:

I was about as religious as one could be. I went to all the church services; I worked in the church; I prided myself on being morally better than most; I prayed and I was a good neighbor. What I didn't know was that all the "good" things I did were my way of saying to God, "Look at me. Aren't you proud of what I've done? I'm sure you won't turn me away from heaven's gates when the time comes."

But I was the only proud one. There would be a day when, at last, I would understand the Scripture, "For by grace you are saved, through faith, and that not of yourselves. It is the gift of God, not of works, lest any man should boast." It wasn't until I quit mentally boasting, realized my total inadequacies before God, and cried out to Jesus to forgive and receive me as His child that I found life and knew it. No longer did I need to trust in any institution or earthly person (including myself) for salvation.

It's believing. It's receiving—inviting Him to come into your life . . . the One who loves you more than any earthly person could. He wants you to be born again, into *His* family.

AS MANY AS RECEIVED HIM, TO THEM GAVE HE POWER TO BECOME THE SONS OF GOD, EVEN TO THEM THAT BELIEVE ON HIS NAME.

What excites me is that I don't need to wait,

wonder, and hope that someday I'll make it, for God has given us a loving assurance:

> THESE THINGS I HAVE WRITTEN TO YOU WHO BELIEVE IN THE NAME OF THE SON OF GOD, THAT YOU MAY KNOW THAT YOU HAVE ETERNAL LIFE.

Amazingly simple, isn't it? No one had to go to a building, do good works, or go through one of His disciples to reach Jesus when He walked the earth in human form. How strange that we insist that one revert to those tactics now! No, salvation is hers when a lady finally realizes that there is nothing she can do to save herself, any more than a drowning child can, and she throws herself upon the mercy of Jesus.

We must be cautious of false beliefs, of course, Carla said, "I thought I ws a Christian. It was my feeling that if I was doing wrong (I had an extramarital affair) God would stop me, but I didn't feel one twinge of guilt. I finally had to face up to the fact that, although I 'believed' in Jesus, so did the devil, but the devil certainly is not going to inherit the kingdom of heaven, for he will not bow down to Jesus' lordship. I was not bowing down to Jesus' lordship either. Once I got that squared away, the step to salvation was a simple one to take. My husband soon followed."

An attorney husband answered my survey with, "My first marriage was without Christ and ended in divorce, in which I lost *everything*—financially, kids, etc. I'm remarried but now I belong to Jesus. He has made everything else wonderful—a constant honeymoon!"

Another husband said, "We have opposite tastes in music, food, movies, books, travel, motels, restaurants . . . but in spite of it all . . . Christ's love and our love for each other makes an impossible situation . . . possible.''

Heart Check

Even if your husband is not inclined to become "born again," don't let that hold you up. Gather your materials for building that castle of a dream marriage. You'll need:

FOR YOUR FOUNDATION
The precious stones of eternal salvation, which are free of charge to you when you surrender to Jesus Christ!

FOR YOUR WALLS
The rare jewels of obeying God in helping your husband act maturely in his responsibilities

FOR AN INPENETRABLE ROOF
Continual praises and thank you's to your heavenly Father, knowing that He will supply in His own time and His own way

FOR YOUR FURNISHINGS
Delicious fresh fruit in every room You'll recognize the varieties—
Love, Joy, Peace of Heart and Mind, Kindness, Goodness, Faithfulness, Gentleness, and Self-Control

To quote Mark Twain, ''Why do you sit there looking like an envelope without an address on it?'' Get your pretty self going. Take that first step toward helping your favorite man become a joy to you and himself. You've little to lose and a household of happiness to gain.

SCRIPTURE REFERENCES